A JUST VERDICT

CAROLINE BARTLETT CRANE
1858–1934

A JUST VERDICT
The Life of
Caroline Bartlett Crane

O'Ryan Rickard

New Issues Press
College of Arts and Sciences

WESTERN MICHIGAN UNIVERSITY

1994

ISBN 0–932826–26–1 *(casebound)*
ISBN 0–932826–27–X *(paperbound)*

Photographs provided by the Regional History Collection,
Western Michigan University Archives,
and the private collection of Julie Durham

Cover Photograph: A photograph taken of Caroline Bartlett Crane during
her ministry at the People's Church in the 1890s.

Frontispiece Photograph: Caroline Bartlett Crane poses for
a picture taken in the early 1890s

Cover design by Linda K. Judy
Photographic assistance by Douglas W. Neal

Printed in the United States of America

To my loving wife,
Joan Bennett Rickard;
my daughter,
Kimberlee,
and my son,
Kyle Ashley

CONTENTS

ILLUSTRATIONS

p. 154—A Savings' Collector takes a small deposit from a woman during the collector's regular rounds. Under Crane's guidance, the Women's Civic Improvement League initiated a savings program to fight loan sharking among the poor in the city.

p. 169—A photograph of "Him" (A. W. Crane) taken from a page in *At the Brown Thrush* written and compiled by Caroline Bartlett Crane as a gift to her husband (from the collection of Crane's grandaughter, Julie Durham).

p. 170—A text page from *At the Brown Thrush.*

p. 188—Minnesota Governor, A. O. Eberhard, fourth person from left on the front row, poses with Caroline Bartlett Crane, at the Minnesota Conservation Congress in St. Paul in 1910. To Caroline's right is Dr. Harvey Wiley, who was the chief chemist of the U. S. Department of Agriculture.

p. 228—"The Children's Year Special" was a special project organized by the Michigan Woman's Committee during World War I. Nurses and physicians examined children brought to the train.

p. 238—Caroline and her adopted children; Bartlett, left, and Juliana, right (from a scrapbook in the collection of Crane's grandaughter, Julie Durham).

p. 239—Dr. A. W. Crane with children (from a scrapbook in the collection of Julie Durham).

p. 244—"Everyman's House" in Kalamazoo was the winner of the 1924 Better Homes design project.

p. 251—A Bas-relief of Caroline Bartlett Crane by Chicago sculptor C. Warner Williams (Regional History Collection, Western Michigan University Archives).

ACKNOWLEDGMENTS

Several people made this project possible. I am most indebted to Dr. Dale Pattison, associate professor of history at Western Michigan University, who suggested this volume and served as my adviser during the early stages of this project. I am grateful also for the assistance of Wayne Mann, director of the Western Michigan University Archives and Regional History Collection, and his staff, Phyllis Burnham, Jeannette Fisher, Mary Witkowski, Barbara Taflinger, and Sue Husband, and the staff of People's Church in Kalamazoo who made archival information available. I also greatly appreciate the insight of Dr. Cynthia Grant Tucker of Memphis State University, who shared with me her research on the Iowa Sisterhood. Heidi Rawson-Ketchum of Western Michigan University libraries, and Catherine Lawson, local history specialist at the Kalamazoo Public Library, also were very helpful. The photos are courtesy of the Western Michigan University Archives. I also would like to thank Ms. Jennifer Syndergaard, who made numerous valuable editorial suggestions.

The primary source for this biography is the Crane Papers, which were presented in 1963 to the Western Michigan University Archives and Regional History Collections, Kalamazoo, Michigan. The collection contains the papers of Caroline Bartlett Crane and of her husband, Dr. A. W. Crane, a pioneer in x-ray technology.

The papers include extensive personal and professional correspondence, sermons, newspaper clippings, published literature, personal journals, notebooks, handwritten notes, speech manuscripts, photographs, and several unpublished typescript autobiographical writings.

The primary source of information about Caroline Bartlett Crane's childhood is a series of typescript recollections written in 1934. These recollections include several small chapters that appear to be a first draft of an autobiography. They include chapters, for example, entitled "My Father," "On *The Viola*," "Le-Claire-Carthage," and "Montrose."

There are two other major unpublished typescript autobiographical articles in the Crane Papers. In 1923, Crane wrote "The Story and the Results," which was never published; it provides an excellent understanding of her childhood and career. Another autobiographical typescript is entitled "Biographical Sketch;" it was written about 1933 by Helen Christine Bennett, a friend and journalist who wrote several articles on Crane.

Although the subject of this biography was born Caroline Julia Bartlett, throughout the manuscript she is called by her professionally known name, Caroline Bartlett Crane. Only during sections relating childhood events and personal events between Crane and her husband, Augustus, is her first name used. These style decisions were made by the writer to avoid gender biases frequently made by writers of biographies about women.

INTRODUCTION

Caroline Bartlett Crane of Kalamazoo, Michigan, ranks among the most significant of the Progressive Era's municipal housekeepers—the women reformers who cleaned up social and sanitation problems in America's industrial cities during the early 1900s. Municipal housekeepers were the environmentalists, consumer advocates, social workers, and community activists of their time. They worked for clean cities with clean air, disease-free food with labels that told the truth, and improved standards of living for children and the poor. Many of them worked, ultimately, for the creation of a just society. Although modern feminists would not support this domestic brand of activism, the municipal housekeepers were in part responsible for breaking down the Victorian barriers that kept women in a separate and inferior society.[1] By claiming that their moral superiority as women uniquely qualified them to be custodians of the public good, municipal housekeepers such as Crane edged their way into the public affairs of a male-dominated society.[2]

As a nationally known, paid consultant on urban problems, Crane differed from municipal housekeepers who led reform projects close to home. Officials from sixty-two cities paid her to visit and tell them what was wrong with their communities. Crane's story is unique, also, in that she did not limit her attention to urban sanitary and sociological problems. Rather, her life is a panoramic mural of the many causes embraced by women's activism between the 1880s and the 1930s, including temperance and the national suffrage movement.

Crane also managed to squeeze in a career as a Unitarian minister at People's Church in Kalamazoo. In an autobiographical sketch, Crane defined this work as her "church ministry" and her efforts as a municipal reformer as her "civic ministry."[3] Her liberal church ministry featured social gospel programs that responded to the impact of industrialization and scientific thought on Protestant Christianity.[4] Her church projects were aimed at improving society through educational opportunities for the working class and blacks.

Crane's interest in social reform was at least partly a product of the remarkable evolution of public attitudes during her lifetime. Born August 17, 1858, in Hudson, Wisconsin, she spent her youth in the "Gilded Age," when Colonel Beriah Sellers, a character created by Mark Twain and Charles Dudley Warner, typified amoral, individualistic Americans during the Grant administration. When Twain and Warner wrote *The Gilded Age,* they had no idea they would label an era (1870–90)—a time of political corruption, fortune-building, and marked transformations of society. It was also during these years that immigrants poured into the country, the great machines of industry belched smoke across the American landscape, and more and more people settled into crowded cities.[5]

During this time the prevailing economic philosophy was the laissez-faire doctrine of Adam Smith and the classical economists—a philosophy that called for unrestrained trade without government interference. The economic climate supported competitive individualism both in corrupt municipal bosses and in tycoons who built huge fortunes and constructed great trusts. Proponents of Smith's theories also created great economic injustice; in this era, social and political historian Harold U. Faulkner claimed, "it was safe to conclude that 80 percent of Americans lived in 1900 on the margin of subsistence while the remaining 20 percent controlled almost the entire wealth of the country."6

Economics aside, the dominant social and philosophical idea of the age was Social Darwinism, a corruption of Charles Darwin's theory of evolution. In *The Origin of Species*, Darwin claimed that societies evolved. It was Herbert Spencer who later tacked on the "survival of the fittest" theory to create Social Darwinism—a belief that man could do nothing to change society and that efforts to reform it would be futile.7

In contrast, Crane's mature years were spent in the Progressive Era, the years between 1890 and 1914, a moralistic age when men and women struggled to perfect a society ripe for repair. The cities of the time were rife with political bosses, crowded tenements, congested traffic, grave health problems, smoky skies, mounds of putrefying garbage, polluted rivers, and a deplorable level of noise. Between the end of the Civil War and the 1920s the portion of the American population that was urban, as opposed to rural, grew from 20 to 51%. In 1920 fifty-four million people lived in the cities and towns of America, compare to only six million in 1860.8 Immigrants and farmers, lured to the cities by jobs in industry, account for most of this amazing growth.9

The enormous problems in the cities offered new opportunities, however, and the 1890s were watershed years for women, especially middle-class women. Cleaning up the cities—municipal housekeeping—emerged as a form of domestic feminism built on the premise that women possessed superior moral qualities that should be applied outside the home. Women turned to civic reform, insisting that the community was an extension of the home and that women should apply their special sensibilities to municipal problems.[10] Men applauded this new role for women. Municipal housekeeping was welcome to take on any civic improvement project that men felt belonged in women's sphere. Noted New York City sanitary engineer George E. Waring said municipal housekeeping was, above all else, "women's work."[11] Although Crane embraced the idea that women had special qualities that suited them for municipal housekeeping, she rejected the belief that women were morally superior.

By the late nineteenth century the theory of female moral superiority was widely accepted in the United States. Reformers believed society could be perfected through the process of evolution and that history moved toward one end—the betterment of humankind. As superior beings, women could help speed that movement. Ironically, the Social Darwinism of an earlier age lent itself to improving the relative prestige of women. Social Darwinists held that women were more highly evolved than men because they lacked animalistic sexual drives and that society would be perfected when men, like women, could live without lust.[12]

The late nineteenth and early twentieth centuries were also times of great optimism. The public believed that science and scientific method could be applied to the study of society and the social sciences. Many social and urban reformers, such as Crane, were certain that if a social problem were studied and understood it could be corrected scientifically. The University of Chicago was at the heart of academic inquiry into the notion that social sciences, applied scientifically, could reform society. Crane completed two sociology courses there in 1896 under institutional charity specialist and sociology professor Charles Henderson.

The University of Chicago, unique as an American school that stressed graduate studies and research, was the home of the world's first department of sociology. Department head Dr. Albion Small was a Baptist minister who had studied the social sciences at the universities in Berlin and Leipzig. In Germany he was influenced by social economists Adolph Wagner and Gustav Schmoller, the founders of *Verein für Socialpolitik*, who believed the social sciences could be used in a scientific manner to repair society.[13]

Crane was influenced by their work and she used Small's *Introduction to a Science of Society* to prepare a Sunday School course titled "Every Day Religion; or Lessons in Good Citizenship,"[14] which was distributed throughout the Western Unitarian Conference. Crane's career as a Unitarian minister was in many ways devoted to reforming society as was her career as an urban reformer. Like other ministers of the social gospel, she developed an "institutional church,"[15] a church inaugurating innovative social programs that neither municipal nor school governments had the foresight to initiate.[16] Crane, like Jane Addams, founder of the Hull House settlement, believed that education was a method for social reform. At People's Church she started a kindergarten, vocational education classes for men and women, and literary and social science discussion groups.[17] She believed that "a church—exempt from taxation—should minister to the needs of—not merely its own members—but, if possible to the unsatisfied needs of the people at large."[18] Crane aspired to make People's Church "an experiment station in social progress."[19] In 1897, with the help of her church members, Crane conducted a sociological survey of Kalamazoo that examined most organizational and community aspects of the small city of twenty-thousand inhabitants. Her project was modeled after the great social surveys of London and Chicago that had been conducted during the previous decade.[20]

During the years that Crane completed courses at the University of Chicago the institution was also a center for the development of sanitary science, which provided the educational base for municipal housekeeping. Marion Talbot came to the university in 1892, first as assistant dean of women and professor of sociology and later as dean of women and head of the department of household administration. In these positions she influenced many young women. She urged students to study a sanitary science (home economics) curriculum that would train them to run their homes and rear their children with a scientific understanding of chemistry, ventilation, textiles, and economics.[21] These young women studied to become efficient, full-time homemakers and mothers. Like many female leaders of her time, Talbot thought women were uniquely qualified as homemakers because of their heightened sensitivities and innately superior morals. College-trained women in particular could draw on these female attributes together with their educations to reform their communities.[22]

Another prominent member of the University of Chicago faculty was John Dewey. By 1900 his "New Education" had received widespread recognition.[23] The result was a change in the focus of education from rote memorization to a more functional approach based on children's anticipated adult occupations. The combination of Dewey's pragmatic and relativistic philosophy and the movement toward industrial education had an important impact on the education of young women. Where traditional education stressed cultural and humanistic courses, New Education employed courses in sanitary science to prepare young women to become homemakers.

The General Federation of Women's Clubs, a national organization established in 1890, also supported home economics education for women. It was a powerful group; by the end of the century it boasted 160,000 members, and by the end of the Progressive Era the federation was one million members strong. Crane served on many national GFWC committees and was a speaker at several national conventions. In 1903 the GFWC created national, state, and local committees to promote home economics education and municipal housekeeping projects. Crane was chairperson of the Michigan Committee for Home Economics. The GFWC created the new committee structure at the urging of the National Household Economics Association, which had been created at the Woman's Congress at the 1893 Chicago World's Fair.

The GFWC played an important part in municipal and social reform because it allowed women to enter public life without abandoning domestic values and without adopting the more radical postures associated with the temperance movement and woman suffrage. The growth in interest in three areas—general home economics, Dewey's practical philosophy, and the GFWC's interest in municipal and social reform and in home economic education for women—combined to increase the popularity of a separate role for women in public life. Across the United States, countless women joined women's clubs and civic improvement leagues such as the Kalamazoo Civic Improvement League organized by Crane. City housekeeping became "quite as much their vocation as taking care of the home;"[24] they believed their families' health and happiness depended in large part on the sanitary conditions of their communities.

Crane completed her church ministry in 1898, and after a brief period to recover from exhaustion she began her work as a civic reformer in earnest, first locally, then statewide, and finally throughout the United States. Between 1906 and 1917 she made sanitary and sociological surveys of dozens of American cities, examining municipal, health, and social services, including water and food supplies, sewage treatment, and school, hospital, and poorhouse conditions. For her, investigation and reform went hand-in-hand. She performed her surveys for the purpose of arousing the public to improve its own institutions and services. Crane marked her success with the results her surveys generated—each new school or cleaner water supply was a victory.[25]

Crane believed public housekeeping to be the most important function of municipal government, and she urged women to assume a share of responsibility for the cleanliness of their cities. She said:

> We certainly should keep our city—that is to say, our common house—clean. The floor should be clean. The air should be clean. The individual houses and premises, the schools, the places of public assembly, the places of trade, the factories, the places where foods are prepared, sold, served, should be clean. There should be sanitary collection and disposal of all the wastes that inevitably accumulate wherever human beings have a home and find habitation.[26]

Among other issues, municipal housekeeping challenged the levels of food hygiene, child welfare, smoke abatement, poorhouse reform, sewage treatment, and meat inspection. Historian Mary Ritter Beard recognized the diversity of the movement in her 1915 volume *Woman's Work in Municipalities*, which includes chapters entitled "Education," "Public Health," "The Social Evil," "Recreation," "Public Safety," "Civic Improvement," and "Government and Administration." Her work is a tribute to the important work of women reformers in large and small towns across America. Crane's civic improvement activities are mentioned prominently in the volume.[27]

The other comprehensive volume on women's civic improvement efforts is *American Women in Civic Work* by journalist Helen Christine Bennett. This book includes biographies of twelve advocates for civic reform, and Crane's is featured in the volume's lead article. For her "sanitary and sociological surveys," Crane earned the title of "America's Public Housekeeper."[28] Journalists described her as a whirlwind of religious zeal who swept into a city to investigate its public institutions and services and then reported on how it could save its civic soul.

Caroline Bartlett Crane died on March 24, 1935. Although a few articles have been written about her since, she has not received her deserved place in history. In her own time, suffragists and social reformers such as Addams received much more press attention than she, and at times Crane was uncertain about the world's reaction to her efforts. An incident in 1909 clearly illustrates her doubt. On October 20, in Richmond, Virginia, she told the American Public Health Association conventioneers that meat inspection had not improved in spite of both new laws enacted in 1906 and new regulations approved as a result of the public outcry over Upton Sinclair's novel, *The Jungle*. Her speech made reference to the contents of confidential internal documents from the Department of Agriculture's Bureau of Animal Industry. She obtained these documents from a meat packing house source in Chicago.[29] The papers were interdepartmental directives to meat inspectors that provided guidelines for interpreting and enforcing government regulations. Crane claimed the documents revealed a conspiracy among meat packers and federal inspectors to lower meat inspection standards. The APHA rejected Crane's disclosures. The motion to create a committee to study her charges was tabled, and she was not allowed to appear before the APHA executive committee to show them her documents. Following her defeat, Crane boarded a train for New York City to ask magazine publishers to print her story.

Before leaving Richmond, she had received a letter of encouragement from her husband, Dr. Augustus Warren Crane. In the letter, he called her "one of the great forces of our day and generation—a civilizing force that will make the world a better place to live in and the people a better race."[30] On the way to New York City, out of frustration and in response to her husband's letters she responded: "That morning had come your blessed letter to stay me with the thought of the verdict of the future on my efforts."[31] She added that the "just verdict of the world" worried her greatly.

Augustus Crane believed that his wife's most significant contribution to society was the expanse of her work. In a letter written earlier in 1909, he said:

> You are universal as are, I believe, all great geniuses. . . . You have only to get these things before the world to be secure as a light for future generations. Your work has breadth denied to settlements because it is for the poor and rich alike. Moreover, it is to improve the things that all have in common that your work aims to do. It seeks to have one big institutional congregation. All the arguments that apply to the institutional church apply to the institutions of towns. [32]

Crane said that although she led both a civic ministry and a church ministry, she considered herself primarily "a preacher." In many ways, she is a projection of the spirit of the reform age, when men and women launched strenuous campaigns to pull moral ideals out of abstraction and into real life. To Crane, religion and good citizenship were one and the same—the ethical duty of every man and woman. She fulfilled her duty through crusades of civic righteousness.

It is unfortunate that the movement by women to improve the quality of city life at the turn of the century was labeled "municipal housekeeping," a designation later feminists would reject. Perhaps the movement would have been better served historically if it had been called "The Women's Civic Improvement Movement," or something similar. Many important volumes on urban history have forgotten this work, reporting only male contributions to urban reform.[33] This biography seeks to direct deserved light on to Caroline Bartlett Crane's work, to pay a tribute to municipal housekeeping as an example of a successful social reform movement, and to render, belatedly and in some small way, the "just verdict of the world."

NOTES

[1]Sara M. Evans, *Born for Liberty: A History of Women in America* (New York: The Free Press, 1989), p. 160.

[2]Karen J. Blair, *The Clubwoman As Feminist: True Womanhood Redefined, 1868–1914* (New York: Holmes & Meier Publishers, 1980), pp. 73–74.

[3]"Biographical Sketch," ca. 1933, unfinished typescript, Crane Papers, Western Michigan University Archives, p. 1.

[4]Charles Howard Hopkins, *The Rise of the Social Gospel in American Protestantism, 1865–1915* (New Haven: Yale University Press, 1940), p. 3.

[5]Harold Underwood Faulkner, *American Political and Social History,* 7th ed. (New York: Appleton-Century-Crofts, 1957), pp. 577–97.

[6]Harold Underwood Faulkner, *Politics, Reform, and Expansion, 1890–1900* (New York: Harper & Row, 1959), p. 91.

[7]Richard Hofstader, *Social Darwinism in American Thought, 1860–1915* (Philadelphia: University of Pennsylvania Press, 1945), pp. 18–36.

[8]Martin V. Melosi, "Environmental Crisis in the City: The Relationship Between Industrialization and Urban Pollution," in *Pollution and Reform in American Cities, 1870–1930,* ed. Martin V. Melosi (Austin: University of Texas Press, 1980), p. 9.

[9]Charles N. Glaab and A. Theodore Brown, *A History of Urban America* (New York: The Macmillan Company, 1967), p. 135.

[10]Blair, *The Clubwoman As Feminist*, pp. 117–20.

[11]George E. Waring, Jr., "Village Improvement Associations," *Scribner's Monthly* 14 (June 1877), 997–98.

[12]Carol Hymowitz and Michaele Weissman, *A History of Women in America* (Toronto: Bantam Books, 1978), p. 219.

[13]Martin Bulman, *The Chicago School of Sociology* (Chicago: University of Chicago Press, 1984), p. 33.

[14]Caroline Bartlett Crane, "Every Day Religion; or Lessons in Good Citizenship," *Old and New* 6 (October 1897), 259–62.

[15]Hopkins, *Rise of the Social Gospel*, p. 154.

[16]Caroline Bartlett Crane, "The Story of the Institutional Church in a Small City," *Charities and the Commons* 14 (6 May 1905), 723–31.

[17]"The Story of the Institutional Church," 723.

[18]"Biographical Sketch," p. 2.

[19]"Biographical Sketch," p. 4.

[20]"A Study of the Social Conditions of Kalamazoo, 1897," handwritten reports, Crane Papers.

[21]Nancy Woloch, *Women and the American Experience* (New York: Alfred A. Knopf, 1984), pp. 286–95.

[22]Bulman, *The Chicago School of Sociology*, pp. 33, 65.

[23]Faulkner, *American Political and Social History,* pp. 720–21.

[24]Suellen M. Hoy, "Municipal Housekeeping: The Role of Women in Improving Urban Sanitation Practices, 1880–1917," in *Pollution and Reform in American Cities*, ed. Melosi, pp. 173–74.

[25]Helen Christine Bennett, *American Women in Civic Work* (New York: Dodd, Mead & Co., 1915), pp. 3–57.

[26]"The Making of an Ideal City," unpublished typescript, Crane Papers.

[27]Mary Ritter Beard, *Woman's Work in Municipalities.* National Municipal League Series (New York: D. Appleton and Co., 1915), pp. 87–88.

[28]*Notable American Women: A Biographical Dictionary,* 4 vols., (Cambridge: Belknap Press of Harvard University Press, 1971–80), s. v. "Caroline Bartlett Crane," 1:402.

[29]Caroline Bartlett Crane, "What Is Happening to American Meat Inspection," unpublished manuscript that claims to be the "substance of a paper given before the American Public Health Association," Crane Papers; U. S. Department of Agriculture, Bureau of Animal Industry, *Service Announcements*, 16 March 1908, 15 January 1908, 15 October 1908, as well as several undated announcements, and photographic copies in Crane Papers; "Documentary Evidence Produced by Mrs. Crane," *The News Leader* (Richmond and Manchester, Va.) (21 October 1909), Crane Papers, Western Michigan University Archives.

[30]Augustus Warren Crane to Caroline Bartlett Crane, 19 October 1909, Crane Papers.

[31]Caroline Bartlett Crane to Augustus Warren Crane, 22 October 1909, Crane Papers.

[32]Augustus Warren Crane to Caroline Bartlett Crane, 18 January 1909, Crane Papers.

[33]See, for example: Charles N. Glaab and A. Theodore Brown, *A History of Urban America* (New York: The MacMillan Company, 1968); Maury Klein, *Prisoners of Progress: American Industrial Cities, 1850–1920* (New York: MacMillan Publishing Co, Inc., 1976); Bayrd Still, *Urban History with Documents* (Boston: Little Brown & Co., 1974). These are just three in a long list of volumes that omit reference to women's contributions.

THE EARLY YEARS

Caroline Bartlett Crane's childhood and adolescence differed from the traditional feminine experience of her time. Her father, Lorenzo Bartlett, was her mentor and stood at the center of Crane's development as a scholarly, strong-willed, and devoutly religious young woman. Crane had a loving relationship with her mother, but it was not the intimate mother-daughter kinship that ordinarily was so central to the life of young women of the nineteenth century.[1] Most mothers trained their daughters for a life of domesticity. But under her father's influence young Caroline studied and read instead of learning how to cook, sew, or sweep the floors.[2]

Caroline learned to read by the age of four, and frequently her father called on her to demonstrate her ability to friends and strangers. On one such occasion, he gave her a book to read for a house guest, but despite her father's prodding Caroline remained speechless. Later, when Lorenzo was alone with his daughter, he spanked her, the only instance of physical punishment she ever experienced.[3] The event was pivotal in Crane's development; her primary motivation through young adulthood was to live up to her father's lofty expectations.

Caroline was Lorenzo's third daughter. He had married Julia Brown in 1849, and they had settled in Ottawa, Illinois, where he worked as a house plasterer. Soon after, Julia gave birth to two girls, Ottilia and Ella, but tragedy touched the family in 1853 when both girls died, apparently of scarlet fever. After their deaths the Bartletts became incredulous of many of the beliefs of orthodox Protestant Christianity. They left the local Methodist Church when its minister brutally comforted them with the notion that their daughters' deaths had been "beneficent providence and God's way."[4] Four years later the Bartletts moved to Hudson, Wisconsin, a small town of about one thousand people situated eighteen miles from St. Paul on Lake St. Croix, a tributary of the Mississippi River. On August 17, 1858, Caroline Julia was born in a white frame house on the lower side of town, near Lake St. Croix.

Following the birth of her brother, Charles, in 1861, Caroline became increasingly attached to her father, mainly because her mother's attention was focused on the infant. When Caroline was eight years old her brother became ill with "bone tuberculosis," a malformation of a hip bone traced to unsanitary milk.[5] In unpublished recollections written in 1934, she said her mother "hovered" over Charles,[6] who recovered only after "six patient years of mother love daily, nightly, hourly ministering."[7] It seems natural that Caroline should have become attached to her father during these early years.

In 1865, Lorenzo purchased a small steamboat, *The Viola*, which carried passengers and freight between St. Paul and St. Louis. For the next six years, he spent most of the warm months on the river. Caroline's happiest moments as a child were spent with her father when he was home during the winter freeze. He talked with his daughter about her schoolwork and discussed the problems she brought to him. Despite his absence for a great part of the year, he continued to play a dominant role in Caroline's development. Instead of being the parent who boasted about her

1.

The house in Hudson, Wisconsin, where Caroline Bartlett Crane was born in 1858.

2.

Caroline's father, Lorenzo Dow Bartlett. The photograph was probably taken around the turn of the century. He died in 1906 in Keokuk, Iowa.

3.

Young Caroline Bartlett is shown with her mother Julia Brown Bartlett.

schoolwork, he became an uncle-like figure who brought lavish presents when he "visited." He became Caroline's hero, a modern knight in shining armor piloting a riverboat down the Mississippi. Two long and three short melodious blasts announced the arrival of *The Viola*. Caroline recalled: "Sometimes I hear them now in my dreams. I hear them now in memory—the most beautiful, enchanting, thrilling clarion call announcing to us—and to all the town—that my papa is coming, my papa is here!"[8] She would run down the street to the landing so she could be in the front of the small crowd that always assembled to welcome the boat home.

Caroline also liked to be the center of attention and to be in charge. She especially enjoyed her little stateroom on *The Viola* and dinners at the Captain's Table with the "important passengers" during summer vacation trips. She gave tours of the boat to other children, explaining the mysteries of capstan and flagstaff. Before their envious eyes, the pilot allowed her to salute passing steamers with an appropriate blast of the whistle. But no spot on *The Viola* held such fascination for her as the pilot house. She would run up the flights of narrow brass-railed stairs to observe minutely the pilot's maneuvers. She often asked him to allow her to take the wheel. At the age of ten, Caroline's wishes finally came true and she piloted *The Viola* for the first time.[9] Caroline quickly became confident of her skills and was allowed to steer the boat on a regular basis, but she soon learned that navigating the Mississippi could be treacherous work. Once at the rapids near Rock Island, Illinois, a pilot ran *The Viola* up on a jagged rock, putting a hole in her bow and creating a panic among passengers and crew. "I shall always admire the cool courage of my father who quickly restored order and directed the filling of the lifeboats with the passengers who looked so funny in their life preservers,"

Caroline recalled. "It was all highly exciting to us children; we had too much confidence in the Captain to be afraid."10

Caroline loved the adventure of the river, but her personality held a quieter side as well. She was unusually sophisticated in her search for philosophical, ethical, and religious truth. Lorenzo and Julia were not so sure of their religious skepticism that they were willing to deprive their children of a religious education, and both Caroline and Charles were sent to the Congregationalist Sunday School.11 Caroline recalled that she took great care in preparing her bible lessons for recitation, but many of the doctrines taught seemed to her a mystery, especially the biblical concept of justice. She could not accept without question the bible stories that portrayed God as cruel and unjust. She also refused to believe that unbaptized infants and heathens were sent to hell. Caroline thought her questions were usually dismissed by adults, whose stock response was "you're not old enough to understand these things."12

During the summer trips on *The Viola*, Caroline spent much of her time at the aft rail creating a secret religious world. She was "given increasingly to meditation and daydreams." "[The] trances," she said, "were induced by the sight and sound of the swirling, foaming water in the steamer's wake." Caroline later recalled that one of the turning points of her life was "that habit of solitary meditation" she developed over the aft rail of *The Viola*.13

By the age of twelve Caroline had rejected traditional Protestant Christianity and the atonement doctrine of salvation. During an illness, she refused to listen to a minister's plan of salvation for her soul, but she had not yet discovered her own faith. It became very difficult for Lorenzo and Julia to talk to Caroline about religious subjects. They became concerned about

4.

Caroline and Charles Bartlett.

her obsession with religion and tried to discourage her introspec-
tiveness.[14]

However, Lorenzo was pleased with Caroline's desire to be
the best student. Classmates, she said, called her the "teacher's
pet," and she made many 100s on her report cards.[15] In
recollections of her childhood Caroline said she believed her
desire to excel was directly related to her desire to please her
father. Lorenzo had attended public school for only three months,
and he was determined that his daughter would receive the
education he never had. He supported her even when her strong
will created problems at school. When she was six years of age the
family moved to a house directly across from the public school on
Vine Street in Hudson. Caroline, who was frequently ill as a child,
returned to school one day after a prolonged illness to find a new
teacher.[16] During recess that day her father summoned her home
to see how she was feeling. Determining that she did not appear
well, he instructed her to tell the teacher that he had asked her to
come home. The teacher became outraged that Caroline had left
the school grounds without permission and refused to allow her to
leave school again. Caroline insisted on obeying her father, and
when the teacher threatened her with a ruler she retaliated by
biting the teacher's arm. An older boy broke up the struggle, and
Caroline fled for home. Her father defended her wholeheartedly
and advised her to return to school the next day to determine
whether she had been expelled. On Caroline's return, the teacher
promptly affirmed the suspension. Lorenzo took the case to the
school board, which reinstated her in school long enough to recite
only once. Then she arrogantly marched out of the school for
good. The remainder of her education in Hudson was in a private
school.[17]

Later Caroline excelled in school in LeClaire, Iowa, where the family moved in 1873. In LeClaire, however, she had difficulty with a male teacher who did not approve of her tendency to show off. He disciplined her when she tried to display her knowledge, calling her behavior "unladylike." Caroline's initiative and strong will were not, apparently, thought properly feminine.[18]

At the age of sixteen Caroline received praise for her independence and intelligence from another quarter when the Bartletts moved to Hamilton, Illinois, at the request of her maternal grandfather, Daniel Brown. Aunt Abigail Haskins lived across the river from Hamilton in Keokuk. Caroline spent many hours talking with her about the liberal Universalist religion and the "tradition of Bartlett women," who, Aunt Abigail said, were strong-willed and independent. Caroline came to see herself as a "Bartlett Woman" like Aunt Abigail and Caroline's grandmother, Ruame, who also was affiliated with the Universalist religion.[19] A favorite family story told how Ruame took her husband's rifle and shot a deer during the family's trek west from New York after the pious John Bartlett, a Baptist, refused to shoot the animal because it was Sunday.

Soon after their arrival in Hamilton, Lorenzo arranged for the Unitarian minister from Keokuk to speak at the City Hall in Hamilton. He wanted to help Caroline work through her doubts about Protestant Christianity, and he insisted that she sit up front behind the preacher instead of with her parents in front of the minister. Reverend Oscar Clute preached a sermon entitled "The Evolution of Religion,"[20] and Caroline remembered that "in this sermon I found all my doubts and problems solved . . . it was like a message from heaven."[21] Caroline fell into a trance after hearing Clute's message that natural progress was the correct way to reconcile the differences between religious beliefs and Darwin's theory of evolution. "I walked out of the place as if in a dream; did not stay to be introduced to the preacher, but escaped in a period of intense exaltation to the refuge of my room." "Later," she said,

> when my father sought for me, in reply to his question as to how I liked the sermon, it must have seemed to him a little like one of my old sleep-walking trances; for I said to him, "Father, I am going to be a Unitarian minister."[22]

Angrily, her father replied, "For Heaven's sake, stop that nonsense. Whoever heard of such an idiotic thing. You're not going to be anything of the kind!" He left her abruptly, unwilling to discuss the issue further.[23] That evening when Caroline went to say good night to her father and mother, she said, "Please remember what I told you, papa. I know that it is my work, and when I am grown up I am going to do it." Again, her parents expressed admonition and distress and assured her that she would "get over it in time."[24] Although he was very advanced in his ideas about education for women, Lorenzo, like Julia, held traditional ideas about the role of woman as wife, mother, and manager of the household.

But Caroline did not "get over it." She knew it was important that she become an excellent orator so she could influence a congregation from the pulpit. At the age of seventeen she demonstrated her ability as a speaker by winning a debate before the Hamilton Philmathean Society.[25] She argued the negative side of the question: "*Resolved* that the Bible should be read in public schools." The debate manuscript reveals that Caroline prepared her case well but still had to overcome the natural prejudice of her listeners, most of whom were white, middle class, and Protestant. She told the audience that it was erroneous to believe that people opposed to reading the bible in schools were heretics who denied the authenticity of the bible. "Justice demands that the bible shall be excluded from the public schools," she said to begin her line of reasoning. "All classes are taxed equally for the support of the schools, and, therefore, all religious exercises should be excluded from them." She argued that it was unjust for Protestants to force Catholics and Jews to hear the Protestant King James version of the bible. Likewise, she said it would be unfair, if the Protestant children were in a minority, for them to have to listen to the Catholic or Jewish versions. In the case of the Muslim children, it would be unjust for Christian or Jewish scripture to be read.

Proud of his daughter's success, Lorenzo became even more determined to provide her with a college education. In Hamilton, Caroline's educational future had been stalemated temporarily by the lack of an accredited public high school. She tried to persuade officials in the accredited school system across the river in Keokuk to allow her to attend, but they refused. Finally, in the summer of 1876, Lorenzo went to Carthage College, in Carthage, Illinois, fourteen miles from Hamilton, and begged officials to admit Caroline.[26] Founded in 1872 by Lutheran ministers, Carthage admitted female students, but they were compelled to take a less strenuous curriculum. Although Caroline had not graduated from high school, Lorenzo successfully argued that his daughter should be admitted because she had completed the required courses.[27] It is quite remarkable that a man who had spent much of his life as a laborer would seek such a lofty opportunity for a son, much less a daughter.

It was not uncommon for the curriculum at coeducational colleges to include inferior courses for women. Carthage officials deleted Greek and calculus from the women's curriculum because they thought the courses were too difficult for the female mind. Upon arrival in Carthage, Caroline immediately challenged the school's academic program. She objected to the watered-down curriculum on two counts: (1) she wanted to take Greek because she believed it would assist her later in seminary when she read New Testament manuscripts; (2) she had already made up her mind that she was going to be the valedictorian of her class, and unless she took the full course of study she would be unable to compete for that honor. Caroline persisted and was successful in persuading the faculty to allow her to take the full classical course of study.[28] To celebrate the victory her father gave Caroline a new Greek dictionary, which he purchased for the outrageous price of $20. She wrote on the flyleaf of the dictionary, "Given me by my father when he could ill afford the expense." Even the wealthiest student would have considered the dictionary a prize.[29]

Education in 1876 was still based on the study of the Roman and Greek classics. The curriculum for first year students, according to the school catalog, included Latin Prose Composition, Cicero's Orations, Livy, Greek Grammar, Xenophon's *Anabasis*, Herodotus, Algebra, Plane Geometry, Solid Geometry, Classical Antiquities, Outlines of History, Physical Geography, Rhetoric, and English Composition.[30] In Caroline's time, there were two hundred students at Carthage College, and the faculty was composed of six professors, all Lutheran ministers, led by the faculty president, Dr. D. L. Tressler, who also served as the professor of mental and moral science. Carthage, the county seat of Hancock County, was a pleasant rural town of about 2,500 inhabitants. The lone college class building stood on a small hill on the outskirts of the town. "It is a large, beautiful, and substantial structure, and is built after the most approved modern

5.

Caroline Bartlett, at age eighteen, when she entered Carthage College.

plans," the catalog reported. In addition to the lecture halls, the building contained a three-thousand volume library and a modern chemistry lab. College officials arranged special boarding rooms for out-of-town students. Caroline's parents paid the significant sum of $150 for Caroline's room and board in a private home for the thirty-five-week term. Tuition was only $25 per year.[31]

As could have been predicted, Caroline's liberal views provoked problems at the Lutheran school. Carthage strictly governed student discipline and observance of religious standards. Students were required to attend chapel service every schoolday morning. Each of the resident students also was expected to attend Sunday religious services at the church of his or her preference or to join faculty at Trinity Lutheran Church. Likewise, resident students were required to attend an hour-long bible study conducted by a member of the faculty each Sunday afternoon.[32]

Caroline became irate when she heard Thomas Paine, the American and French revolutionary hero, denounced during chapel services as "a filthy little atheist." Paine, the chief prophet of deism in America, popularized skepticism of superstitious Christianity.[33] He and other deists denied the possibility of a revealed religion in which humanity was handed truths from a divine being. Instead, deists contended, there was a natural religion that was commonly known through reason by all humanity.[34] Caroline announced that she would not attend chapel as long as the opinions of liberal men such as Paine were condemned. She was, of course, called before the faculty, and stubbornly, she reiterated her determination not to listen to such lectures or to sing conservative hymns. President Tressler told her that she could not attend classes unless she attended chapel, but the threat only hardened Caroline's persistence and indignation. One cold evening a few days later Tressler called upon Caroline at her boarding house. It would have been inappropriate for him to come inside, so he summoned her outside. Caroline shook in the freezing air; it was so cold she could hardly open her mouth to speak. President Tressler was kind but firm in his declaration that she must attend chapel. Caroline simply said, "I can't and I won't!"

To her great surprise, he replied, " 'We'll let this matter rest. I feel sure that you will think better of your determination.' " She did not go to chapel the next morning, or the next. Several days passed and she heard nothing more about expulsion. Then one of her classmates told her that the tone of chapel addresses had changed, and Caroline decided of her own free will to return. She continued to attend chapel and from that point forward never again heard Paine criticized.[35]

At Carthage, Caroline continued to hone her skills as an orator by participating in literary society debates and speaking on behalf of the temperance cause. During the summers she took special classes to complete the equivalent of five years of Greek in three years. She later blamed her Greek studies for her poor eyesight. Caroline would arise at three o'clock in the morning and study her Greek lessons by kerosene lamp.[36]

The young student learned only a week before graduation in the spring of 1879, that she would indeed be valedictorian. Caroline's mother feverishly made her graduation dress of black silk. It had a ruffled overskirt with a bouffant effect in the back. Her parents gave her a gold watch for graduation—which Caroline placed in the pocket of her new dress.[37] A classmate helped her put her hair up in a stylish French twist. In her valedictory address, entitled "Our Ideals," Caroline stressed the possibility of perfectionistic ethics, reasoning that an ideal standard of perfection was probably unattainable but if her classmates and she set their ideals high, they would strive harder, and therefore, rise higher. A newspaper account said that her "language was elegant, her enunciation was beautifully distinct, and her style of delivery very effective."[38] She had earned her bachelor's degree in only three years and attained her goal of being valedictorian. However, her goal of becoming a minister seemed distant. Meadville Theological Seminary, a Unitarian seminary located in Meadville, Pennsylvania, admitted female students, but her father would not relent in his opposition and give her financial assistance; and churches, even in the more liberal West, did not provide scholarships for women as they did for male students.[39]

As graduation approached she had no idea what she would do after college. She gave some thought to lecturing and to teaching elocution (a combination of diction, oral interpretation, and speech) to private students. President Tressler had suggested, as he did to most women graduates, that Caroline teach in a public or private school. Although denied the ministry, she was determined to have a career.[40]

In April, a month before graduation, Tressler had called her to his office and shown her a letter from a Montrose, Iowa, school board member who wanted the president's help in securing a school principal for the town, which was located about twenty miles north of Hamilton.[41] Caroline accepted the position, but after only one year in Montrose she returned home. Montrose was a riverboat town, and many of the male students were older because they attended school only when they were not working. On one occasion, Crane had to take a gun away from an older student.

However, she still did not have the courage to strike out on her own without the consent of her father. Crane's sickness of soul was accompanied by physical sickness. Her health was getting worse. She apparently suffered from iron-deficiency anemia and high blood pressure. After the Montrose experience, she decided to turn to teaching elocution to private students—primarily out of desperation for a career—instead of teaching gun-carrying river youths. To provide herself with better professional credentials she went to Chicago in the fall of 1880, to take private elocution lessons at the Central Music Hall. But Caroline was not satisfied with her life.[42] After about six months of study she suddenly quit her speech lessons and took a job as a reporter for the *Chicago Telegraph* in April 1881.[43] Crane wrote her parents that she enjoyed the job, and she would explain to them later, when she visited home, why she had quit her speech lessons. But by summer, for some unknown reason, she had quit the newspaper job, also, and returned home. Her mother suffered greatly during this period, and on February 19, 1883, died of gallstones. Charles, Caroline, and Lorenzo grieved deeply. In their mourning, Lorenzo and Caroline decided not to remain in Keokuk with their memories but to file a homestead claim in Dakota Territory, which had recently been opened up for land claims. So in early April 1883 Crane and her father left for Dakota Territory. (Charles had returned to his railroad job shortly after Julia's death.) Their trek ended when they arrived at Ellendale, just a few miles north of what would become the South Dakota-North Dakota state line. At Ellendale they hired a prospector who helped them locate a homestead site.[44]

Crane's health improved, and in the fall of 1883 she went to the Minneapolis-St. Paul area in search of a place to live and work. After several unsuccessful tries, in December 1883 she gained an interview with the city editor of the *Minneapolis Tribune*. Charles Aft Williams did not especially like women reporters, but he was impressed by Crane's persistence. He also knew that Crane, like other women reporters, would work for a lower wage than a man, so he hired her at the salary of five dollars weekly.[45] Crane told Williams that she was willing to do the work done by any man, and she insisted that she be given general assignment reporting duties, instead of being assigned to write women's news only. She did not get her wish for general reporting immediately. On a regular basis she was assigned such menial reporting tasks as copying real estate records at the courthouse, and in January 1884 she was assigned to the religious, educational, and benevolent beat, where she chiefly wrote music and drama reviews.[46] She was the only woman newsperson of about one hundred journalists on the four area newspapers.[47] On this beat she became friends with the three Unitarian ministers in the Twin Cities area—the Reverends William Channing Gannett, Samuel McChord Crothers, and Henry M. Simmons—and she let them know that she wanted to become a liberal minister. During her newspaper work, she said, she did not lose sight of her real aim. Under the guidance of the Reverend Oscar Clute, at that time the Minnesota Unitarian Conference missionary, and the three ministers, she continued to study for the ministry.

Crane enjoyed interviews more than any other task. Her most important was with writers Mark Twain (Samuel Clemens) and George W. Cable. She interviewed them on Saturday evening, January 24, 1885, before their public readings.[48] Another reporter had been sent to interview the writers, but Twain declined, so she volunteered to try her hand. When Crane arrived at the hotel she sent her card up to their room with the message: "Would Mr. Clemens kindly grant an interview with a young woman who has had considerable experience as a Mississippi River pilot?" This changed the situation. It was now Twain, former river pilot, who wanted to talk to Crane. Twain, she said, was skeptical of her claim and was determined to flush out this charlatan. "Did you cabin in the texas?" Twain asked.

"Yes, my father was captain of the boat, all the officers, of course, had quarters in the texas," she replied. (The texas was the uppermost level of a steamboat, usually to the rear of the pilot house.) Crane had given the correct answer. Twain then made some reference to the hurricane deck in a further attempt to trick her. She refused to fall for Twains claim that the hurricane deck had something to do with hurricanes or that there was any such thing. Twain was not easily persuaded. He felt that she would not know anything about navigating a steamboat, so in the middle of what purported to be a reply to one of Crane's questions about his Mississippi River steamboat days he said: "You know when two steamboats meet, the one going upstream always has the choice of sides." To which Crane shook her head unbelievingly. Twain laughed and said, "I give up!"[49] She got her interview and no longer was considered a green reporter; she had succeeded where a more experienced reporter had failed. She enjoyed this ingeniously won prestige for some time, she said, before disclosing that her personal experience on the river had given her the advantage.

In addition, Crane interviewed such public figures as Belva Lockwood, the so-called "Queen of the American Bar," and Lucy Stone, the leader and founder of the American Woman Suffrage Association.[50] In 1872, Lockwood had become the first woman to be granted permission to practice law before the United States Supreme Court. When Crane interviewed her she was a candidate for President of the United States, although most people did not take her candidacy seriously. When Crane asked her why she was running, she jokingly replied: "When I was ten years old I read the Old Testament and the New Testament through, and straightway I tried to perform every one of the miracles!"

Crane interviewed Stone on the eve of the 1885 AWSA convention in Minneapolis. Under the pseudonym "Nell Hudson," Crane in August 1885 began writing a regular column dealing with women's social and civic issues.[51] (Crane had expressed compassion for a little retarded classmate in Hudson named "Nellie."[52]) In a "Nell Hudson" column written during the convention, Crane said she believed that education was more important for women than the vote, and she blamed apathetic women for the failure of colleges to create opportunities for them to be educated and practice the professions such as medicine, law, and the ministry. She also rejected the commonly held Victorian idea that women were morally superior to men. Leaders of the suffrage organizations and the Women's Christian Temperance Union argued that, if given the vote, women would eliminate the evils of society which were mainly attributable to men. She wrote:

> And there are bad women as well as good women, although we never hear any word about it from the reformers. One would suppose that the solid woman vote could always be counted on to drop in favor of pure law and order and morality, but there are indifferent women, and fanatical women, and women obstructionists, and a great army of deliberately bad women.[53]

If exposed to the same temptations as men, Crane said, it would be clear that the sexes, morally speaking, were equal.

Meanwhile, Crane began to handle more difficult news stories and at times was given the opportunity to work the city editor's desk as an assistant. She had been at the newspaper for almost two years when Williams received a letter advising him that the Oshkosh (Wisconsin) Morning Times needed a city editor to be in charge of all its local news. Oshkosh was a tough logging town, and, according to Williams, it was not out of place for the city editor of the newspaper to carry a revolver and to keep his body in good shape. Large, two-fisted men frequently came to the newspaper office and "cleaned out the establishment," he said. No one on the *Tribune* staff showed an immediate interest. Crane read the letter and suggested that if Williams would write her a letter of recommendation she would take the position. The staff was amazed, but Williams and Crane convinced the Oshkosh publisher that she was a "thorough newspaper man."[54] She began her work in Oshkosh in November 1885, supervising three male reporters who on many occasions drank heavily and were not able to work. This did not sit well with Crane, who boasted that she represented the fifth generation of a family of "tee-totallers," nor did their profanity sit well. She advised the reporters that she would not endure their cursing, and if it did not cease she would dismiss the offenders.[55]

Life in Oshkosh was quite hectic. Crane had never been in a lumbering town, and she was in no way prepared for the boisterous night life of Oshkosh's streets. The newspaper did not go to press until four o'clock in the morning, and the late press time meant that much of Crane's work was done at night. She said she carried a loaded revolver with her but was almost as scared of the gun as of the people it was presumed to protect her from; she had no idea how to fire the revolver.[56] At the time, Crane believed that she was the only woman with the rank of city editor of a daily newspaper in the United States.[57] This claim has not been confirmed, but it is evident that she was one of the few women in the United States in 1885 with such a high ranking newspaper position. Crane took the job because she wanted to run a news department, but in the spring of 1886 she realized that the

6.

A photograph taken of Caroline Bartlett Crane around 1888.

work was not moving her toward her purpose—to be a minister—so she resigned her position and returned to her father's home in Dakota Territory and once again sought his blessing.

Her father was glad to see her and constructed a little two-room shack for her, about a mile from his house, on a homestead claim she filed in her own name.[58] Since she had left home her father had married Louise Babcock of Delaven, Wisconsin. Crane did not clarify her true intentions immediately. Finally she got up enough courage and asked him for his blessing again as they rode from Ellendale in a buggy to their home on the deserted frontier: "Father, I've got to tell you something. I am going to enter the Unitarian ministry as soon as I leave here in the fall."

She recalled that her father's reply seemed to take an eternity. "My dear, you have held to this idea for a very long time. God bless you. And if I can help you in any way, I'll do it."[59]

NOTES

[1] Caroll Smith-Rosenberg, "The Female World of Love and Ritual: Relations between Women in Nineteenth-Century America," in *Women's Experience in America: An Historical Anthology*, eds. Esther Katz and Anita Rapone (New Brunswick, Conn.: Transaction Books, 1980), pp. 259–91. (Reprinted from *Signs* 1 [1975], 1–29).

[2] Caroline Bartlett Crane, "Early Home and Schooldays," p. 4, in 1934 typescript recollections, Crane Papers.

[3] Crane, "Brother Charles," p. 6, in 1934 typescript recollections, Crane Papers.

[4]Caroline Bartlett Crane, "My Father," p. 6, in 1934 typescript recollections, Crane Papers.

[5]Caroline Bartlett Crane, "My Mother—and the Little Girl Next Door," *Woman's Journal* 23 (May 1914), 165. (Transcript of speech given at a suffrage rally in Kalamazoo, Michigan, 2 May 1914.)

[6]Crane, "Brother Charles," p. 1.

[7]Handwritten notes, 2 May 1897, Crane Papers.

[8]Crane, "On *The Viola*," p. 1, in 1934 typescript Recollections, Crane Papers.

[9]Crane, "On *The Viola*," p. 3; and "The Story and the Results," p. 3, ca. 1923 typescript autobiographical sketch, Crane Papers.

[10]Crane, "On *The Viola*," p. 5.

[11]Crane, "My Father," p. 6, in 1934 typescript recollections, Crane Papers.

[12]Crane, "My Early Religious Struggles," p. 1, in 1934 typescript recollections, Crane Papers.

[13]Crane, "The Story and the Results," p. 4.

[14]Crane, "The Story and the Results," p. 6.

[15]LeClaire City Schools report card, 1874, Crane Papers.

[16]Crane, "Early Home and Schooldays," pp. 5–6, in 1934 typescript recollections, Crane Papers.

[17]Crane, "Early Home and Schooldays," pp. 5–6.

[18]Crane, "LeClaire-Carthage," p. 1, in 1934 typescript recollections, Crane Papers.

[19]Crane, "My Father," p. 8; and Crane, "The Story and the Results," pp. 1–2.

[20]Crane, "My Early Religious Struggles," pp. 2–3.

[21]Crane, "My Early Religious Struggles," p. 3; and Frances E. Willard and Mary A. Livermore, eds., *A Woman of the Century,* s. v. "Caroline Bartlett" (Buffalo, New York: Charles Wells Moulton, 1893; reprint by Gale Research Company, Detroit, Michigan, 1967), pp. 59–60.

[22]Crane, "My Early Religious Struggles," p. 3.

[23]Crane, "My Early Religious Struggles," p. 3; and Crane, "The Story and the Results," p. 7.

[24]Crane, "My Early Religious Struggles," p. 3.

[25]Caroline Bartlett Crane, "The Bible Should Not Be Read in Public Schools," unpublished handwritten debate manuscript prepared for delivery before the Philmathean Society, Hamilton, Illinois, 31 March 1876, Crane Papers.

[26]Crane, "Early Home and Schooldays," p. 8.

[27]Crane, "LeClaire-Carthage College," p. 2.

[28]Crane, "LeClaire-Carthage College," p. 2.

[29]Crane, "Early Home and Schooldays," p. 11.

[30]*Catalogue of Carthage College*, Carthage, Illinois, 1878–79, Crane Papers.

[31]*Catalogue of Carthage College.*

[32]Crane, "LeClaire-Carthage College," p. 3.

[33]Thomas Paine, *Age of Reason. Being an Investigation of True and Fabulous Theology.* Reprint ed. (New York: Willey Book Company, 1965, originally published in 1794), passim.

[34]*Deism and Natural Religion: A Source Book*, E. Graham Waring, ed., with introduction by E. Graham Waring (New York: Frederick Ungar Publishing Co., 1967), pp. ix–x.

[35]Crane, "LeClaire-Carthage College," p. 4.

[36]Crane, "LeClaire-Carthage College," p. 3.

[37]Caroline Bartlett Crane, "Memories of C. C.," *Carthage College Bulletin* 9 (September 1925), no page numbers, Crane Papers.

[38]Untitled, unidentified newspaper, undated, Nell Hudson Scrapbooks, and Carthage College 1879 Graduation Program, Crane Papers. (There are two Nell Hudson scrapbooks, so designated because they contain several clippings signed "Nell Hudson," the *nom de plume* used by Caroline Bartlett while a newspaper reporter and editor in Oshkosh, Wisconsin, and Minneapolis. The scrapbooks contain newspaper clippings that date from 1876 to 1896.)

[39]Caroline Bartlett, "The Liberal Minister: His Equipment and Place," pamphlet containing transcript of a sermon delivered at the Western Unitarian Conference meeting in the Memorial Baptist Church in Chicago, 18 May 1892, Crane Papers.

[40]Caroline Bartlett Crane, "Montrose," p. 1, in 1934 typescript recollections, Crane Papers.

[41]Caroline Bartlett Crane, "Montrose," p. 1.

[42]Crane, "Notes," p. 2, in 1934 typescript recollections, Crane Papers.

[43]Caroline Bartlett to Lorenzo and Julia Bartlett, 12 April 1881; and Caroline Bartlett to Lorenzo and Julia Bartlett, 23 April 1881, Crane Papers.

[44]Caroline Bartlett Crane, "Ellendale," p. 1, in 1934 typescript recollections, Crane Papers.

[45]"The Pastor of the People's Church: Recollections of Her as a Newspaper Worker in Minneapolis by Her City Editor," *Cincinnati Commercial-Gazette* (2

February 1896), Nell Hudson Scrapbooks, Crane Papers. (The article was written by Charles Aft Williams, Crane's city editor at the *Minneapolis Tribune*.)

[46]Untitled article, *Minneapolis Tribune*, Nell Hudson Scrapbooks, Crane Papers. ("January, 1884" is written on the clipping.)

[47]"The Pastor of the People's Church: Recollections of Her as a Newspaper Worker in Minneapolis by Her City Editor."

[48]"An Interesting Chat with Clemens and Cable Upon Their Work," *Minneapolis Tribune* (25 January 1885; Microfilm Reproduction, St. Paul: Minnesota State Historical Society).

[49]Michigan Authors Association, *Proceedings of the 12 May 1928 Meeting of the Michigan Authors Association*, by Caroline Bartlett Crane, Benton Harbor, Crane Papers; "Will Never Be Forgotten," *Michigan Tradesman*, undated, Crane Papers.

[50]"A Spicy Interview," *Minneapolis Tribune*, undated, Nell Hudson Scrapbooks, Crane Papers.

[51]"Society Doings," *Minneapolis Tribune* (23 August 1885; Microfilm Reproduction, St. Paul: Minnesota State Historical Society.)

[52]Caroline Bartlett Crane, "Nellie," p. 1, in 1934 typescript recollections, Crane Papers.

[53]Caroline J. Bartlett (Nell Hudson), "This Week Socially: Equal Rights," *Minneapolis Tribune* (25 October 1885; Microfilm Reproduction, St. Paul: Minnesota State Historical Society).

[54]"The Pastor of the People's Church: Recollections of Her as a Newspaper Worker in Minneapolis by Her City Editor."

[55]Caroline Bartlett Crane, "Oshkosh," p. 2, in 1934 typescript recollections, Crane Papers.

[56]Crane, "Oshkosh," p. 2.

[57]Crane "Oshkosh," p. 1; and the *Oshkosh Sunday Times*, 1885 and 1886. (Microfilm Reproduction, Madison, Wisconsin: Wisconsin State Historical Society.)

[58]Crane, "My Early Religious Struggles," p. 5.

[59]Crane, "My Early Religious Struggles," p. 5.

THE CHURCH MINISTRY

Crane had returned to the treeless Dakota prairie when she was twenty-seven years old. While bathed in solitude there, she spent her time meditating and writing sermon-length answers to personal theological questions, such as, Why do I believe in God? Why do I believe in immortality? What do I believe about Jesus? What is the bible to me? What should a liberal church mean to a community?[1] When she completed a sermon, she would send it to one of her minister friends for his reaction. She prized Reverend Clute's advice most highly. Crane's theological work was flavored heavily with the transcendentalism of Ralph Waldo Emerson, who held that through mystical inner experiences, men could come to know the universal God. Other theologians she considered important were the Reverend Minot Judson Savage, a Chicago Unitarian minister, and the important Unitarian thinkers William Channing and Theodore Parker. In the isolation of her shack on the plains of Dakota, Crane said that she never felt so near to "the heart of things."[2]

With her father's approval granted at last, Crane wrote to Clute in the fall of 1886 that she was determined to become a liberal minister. Liberalism, like the adjective "liberal," denotes an openness to divergent opinions and the desire for intellectual liberty. American liberal theologians wanted to liberate religion from traditional theological creeds that stressed the supernatural so as to give man's moral and rational powers wider scope.[3] She told Clute that she could not conscientiously identify herself with the Universalists or with any other denomination, "except it be the Unitarian," primarily because Unitarians did not require the acceptance of a creed. She wrote:

> I understand that the Unitarian body allows for all progress in belief and fixes no creed either for its members or its ministers. What I want to do is this: In as simple a way as possible, to help each people as are in need of a rational basis for religious faith; and to show them that such a faith may be best won and sustained by living a rational life.[4]

Crane added that she considered herself "very far from the most conservative side of Unitarianism," which was the American vanguard for liberal theology in the nineteenth century. But she said she would always "for myself and my ministry to keep the name of Christian, not under constraint, but because I love, though I could not insist that others must acknowledge themselves of Jesus before they can begin a religious life."

On October 18, ten days after the writing of this letter, Crane presented herself to the Iowa State Unitarian Conference meeting in Des Moines and was accepted as a candidate for the ministry. The zealous Iowa Unitarian Conference of the 1870s and 1880s led the denomination in ordaining women ministers. Women ministers had started moving into the male ranks of the Unitarian ministry after the Civil War, but by the 1880s only a handful of women ministers had been ordained. According to the 1880 census, only 165 women ministers served in all denominations in the United States.[5]

In the 1880s ordination of Unitarian women ministers was strictly a western phenomenon. In the East, American Unitarian

Association leaders believed that women belonged in the church kitchen or in Sunday School instead of in the pulpit. They deemed women unfit for high church positions that demanded business skills. Church officials in the East believed that if women were allowed to serve there, they would displace qualified men. But in the West the missionary effort was short of male ministers. Many of the western congregations were so small they could not pay the salary a male minister needed to support a family. Church officials assumed that women ministers would remain unmarried, and, therefore, that their material needs would be smaller.[6] The label "Iowa Sisterhood" referred to the women ministers who worked in the Iowa conference or began their ministry there. When Crane presented herself to the Iowa conference the sisterhood had five members, of whom the most prominent were also its unofficial leaders—Mary Safford and Eleanor Gordon. Safford and Gordon were also from Hamilton, Illinois, and had started their ministry there in 1878. They were influenced by Clute in much the same way that Crane had been. In their hometown, Crane had not been an intimate friend of Safford or Gordon, both of whom were six years older than she. The duo had moved in 1880 to Humboldt, Iowa, which was to become the center of the Iowa Sisterhood work. Their base of operation was a five-room apartment on the upper floor of an old farmhouse near the Humboldt Unity Church. Safford served as pastor, and Gordon was the high school principal.[7] Most of the members of the sisterhood were unmarried, and it was not uncommon for a pair of the sisters to serve a church as a team.

With Clute's help, church trustees of the All Souls Unitarian Church in Sioux Falls, Dakota Territory, named Crane their minister on January 1, 1887.[8] Because of her lack of theological training, Crane was considered an unordained novice by Iowa Conference officials, but Sioux Falls needed a preacher: the Reverend Eliza Tupper Wilkes, a Universalist minister who worked closely with Unitarians, had founded the congregation in Sioux Falls but then wanted freedom to leave town to found additional churches.

Upon her arrival Crane was asked to take charge of a campaign to construct a building while Wilkes went East to seek missionary funds from the American Unitarian Association in Boston. Prior to Crane's arrival, the small congregation had met in the law office of Wilkes's husband, and during the early months of her tenure the congregation rented an adventist church building.[9]

Crane wanted the new church's design to reflect her personal theology. She did not care for the cold, formal architecture of orthodox churches; instead, she believed that a church's design should provide a comfortable, homelike setting for its members and programs. Furthermore, Crane held that female ministers should "make the whole world homelike," a "feminine theology" not uncommon among the sisterhood. Mary Safford, for example, wanted to be known by her Humboldt, Iowa, church as its "mother" and enjoyed the fact that her work as a minister sometimes meant that she preached and swept floors, paid bills and waited on tables.[10]

Church members accepted Crane's proposed design, and on February 22, 1888, they occupied the new building for the first time. A newspaper editor probably under Crane's influence wrote:

> A cheerful fire in the parlor grate gave the church a home air which instantly and almost insensibly removed the strained feeling which destroys the natural actions of and lends a self-conscious expression to the face of periodical church-goers.[11]

The external appearance of the church shocked the community, the majority of whom thought it looked like a large house. Indeed, the structure did not look much like a church: it had no steeple or stained-glassed windows. In her first sermon in the new building, which had a seating capacity of two hundred, Crane pleaded with the membership to make the church a place of service for the community, not merely a meeting place for the membership. "Do you see there are no steeples and Gothic riches pointing solemnly heavenward?" she said. "Our little church nestles lovingly down to earth, as if it knew it belonged there and loved its mission in this work-a-day world." "People say it doesn't look like a church," she proudly acknowledged. "Everyone who views it from the outside remarks that it looks like a home. . . ."[12] In her sermon Crane revealed for the first time an interest in Social Christianity. She told the congregation:

> . . . this church cannot be a place where we are merely to come together once a week and enjoy our doctrine and congratulate ourselves that we have a faith free from superstition. We must do something for others as well as for ourselves. And the more we have done for others, the more in the end, we shall find we have done for ourselves.[13]

A submovement within religious liberalism, the Social Gospel was a response to industrialism and urbanization that involved nearly all Protestant denominations, but it grew most vigorously among Unitarians, Congregationalists, and Episcopalians.[14] The Social Gospel rested upon a few dominant ideas. Among these were: (1) the immanence or indwelling of God working out His purposes in the world of men; (2) the organic or solidarist view of society, which was conveniently supplied by the new social science of sociology; and (3) the presence of the kingdom of heaven on earth.[15] Under the influence of Social Gospel teachings and of Emerson, Crane rejected supernatural Christianity. Her sermons reveal she believed in the existence of God in the immanent, Emersonian sense and in the immortality of the soul. She also believed, as Emerson did, that the Oversoul—the ultimate reality of a natural or rational religion—was inherent in the world and could be found through man's consciousness and experience.[16]

For Crane, and other advocates of the Social Gospel, the doctrine of the immanence of God broke down the traditional distinctions between the sacred and the secular. They believed God lives through all the ranks of creation; therefore, He must dwell in natural processes that could provide man with moral ideals to improve the processes of human society. In a sermon published by her Sioux Falls church Crane said:

> And then, as men went on further into the light, there came somehow the conviction that moral force is the one indestructible force in the universe; that it somehow pervades all other forces; that the planets running their courses, and the seed sprouting from the ground, and the bird sitting patient upon its nest, and the human being doing an act of justice or mercy to his fellow-man or beast—all were obeying the law laid upon them by that Higher Power that makes for righteousness; and that obedience is the fulfilling of the moral law; nay that obedience is worship—blind, unconscious, in the star, the tree, the bird; active, knowing, rejoicing obedience and worship in the soul of man.[17]

Like other Social Gospel advocates, Crane was influenced by Darwin's theory of evolution, which links moral and religious ideas to the contemporary optimistic belief in progress. Evolution's chief value, she believed, was not to explain the existence of life but to provide a new understanding of the methods of life.[18]

In numerous sermons Crane reported that man's understanding of moral ideas evolved with each century. She thought that the life of Abraham Lincoln had as much or more moral value as the life of the Hebrew Abraham.[19] Although she revered Jesus Christ, she held that he was no more divine than any other man or woman who performed God's will.[20]

Meanwhile, in the 1880s, a controversy called "The Western Issue" embroiled liberal and conservative Unitarians. Would the church remain theistic in the traditional Christian sense or would it reject the necessity of any creed and accept only "freedom, truth, and right living" as the basis for religion? The eastern establishment—the American Unitarian Association—supported the theistic position. At a meeting of the Western Unitarian Conference in Cincinnati in 1886, however, the liberal secularists won the doctrinal war, stating there would be no theistic dogmatic tests for membership.[21]

The Western Unitarian Conference covered an area of what would eventually become sixteen Midwest and Western states. The Reverends Jenkin Lloyd Jones and William Channing Gannett led the liberal movement. During the summer of 1888, Crane spoke at Jones's All Souls Church in Chicago. Jones, formerly the chief executive of the Western Unitarian Conference, had been the most instrumental figure in the ordination of women into the Iowa ministry. He pastored what he called a "seven day" church that was open for community-oriented activities every day, instead of being mainly a place of Sunday worship. Jones's concepts influenced Crane's ministry.[22]

The Western Unitarian Conference widely distributed two of Crane's most popular sermons: *Creeds: Their Use and Abuse,* and *Truths and Errors in Col. Ingersoll's Method and Argument.* In the first, Crane vigorously opposed mandatory religious creeds.

"Every earnest Unitarian has a creed," she said. "People don't amount to much unless they have personal creed." She added that it was wrong to force one's personal creed on someone else.[23] Her second much-read sermon was a response to the so-called "Ingersoll-Black-Field-Gladstone-Manning Debate," the most widely publicized religious controversy of the late 1880s, which involved Colonel Robert Ingersoll, the foremost critic of Christian theology. Ingersoll and three orthodox Christian clergy members wrote a series of articles in the *North American Review* debating Ingersoll's criticism of orthodox religion.[24] Ingersoll had been a colonel in the Union army, a highly successful trial lawyer, and a political figure best remembered for the "Plumed Knight" oration with which he nominated James G. Blaine as the Republican presidential candidate in 1876. The son of a conservative Protestant minister, he devoted his mature life to the cause of agnosticism in religion. In his lectures Ingersoll outlined centuries of criminal-like activities of so-called churchmen. In her sermon, Crane praised Ingersoll's attacks on superstitious Christianity but claimed it was entirely unfitting for him to accuse Christianity of every crime that had been perpetrated by one of its members.

The membership of the Sioux Falls church grew from 70 to 250 members during Crane's tenure.[25] She counted as her greatest success, however, the organization of a Unity Club. Unity Clubs were commonplace among Unitarian churches during this period. They claimed to be community-wide and non-sectarian and were usually involved in group academic studies and community projects.[26] Crane appears to have been restrained from instituting more liberal programs in Sioux Falls because of her need to obtain American Unitarian Association church mission moneys for the building fund. During the dispute over the

"Western Issue," the AUA cut off funds from new mission churches in the West that were not theistic.[27] A $1,500 AUA loan partially funded the new Dakota church.[28]

Although the leaders of the Iowa Sisterhood were active suffragists, no evidence exists to indicate that Crane became active in the suffrage cause at this time. But during her ministry in the Dakota Territory she did continue her support of the temperance campaign, taking a leadership role in a local crusade. The Women's Christian Temperance Union (WCTU), it should be noted, was active in the suffrage cause. Its leaders believed that if women got the vote, they would provide the needed votes in temperance referendums.

Meanwhile, in January 1889, Crane advised the trustees of the Sioux Falls church that she planned to resign to further her theological studies, possibly at the Chicago Theological Seminary.[29] When John Effinger, general secretary of the Western Unitarian Conference, heard that Crane planned to leave the Sioux Falls church, it immediately occurred to him that she could study in Chicago during the week and travel the 140 miles eastward to Kalamazoo, Michigan, to preach on the weekends. The Kalamazoo congregation had been troubled for several years and had been without a minister for five years. Church records do not reveal the cause of the dispute among its members.

Reverend Gannett agreed to preach in Sioux Falls for Crane on March 17, 1889, while she traveled to Kalamazoo. She was met at the Kalamazoo train station by three church members who were hospitable but who did not relish the task of entertaining her. The church leaders were not happy that Effinger had sent a woman preacher. This was not Iowa, and women ministers were rare in Michigan. According to an 1884 Michigan census, there were 707 male and only 6 female ministers.[30] Crane's hosts explained that the church had not had a full-time minister since 1883, and no Sunday School had been held since 1885. The sad condition of the church sparked Crane's interest.

To her surprise, the little white frame church was nearly filled on Sunday morning.[31] Church leaders had given advance notice that a woman would be speaking, and, although several members had threatened to boycott the service, their curiosity prevailed. In fact, many non-members came to see this unusual visitor. She was an immediate success. A newspaper report said that Crane's "powerful exposition" in the morning service attracted an even larger crowd that night. "The lady is a pleasing speaker, has a tall commanding figure, and her words carry conviction by reason of her earnestness," the report added.[32] That evening she delivered the sermon on Ingersoll. "Miss Bartlett's evening audience was one of the largest ever gathered in the church and the impression she created was excellent," the newspaper said.

It took two meetings with the trustees and another trip to Kalamazoo before Crane accepted the pastorate at a $1,000 annual salary. Before she accepted, however, the trustees agreed that she would be allowed to attend classes in Chicago during the week, that she would be allowed to select the hymns for the worship services, and that at least one woman would be named to the board of trustees.[33]

Before taking her new pastorate in Kalamazoo, Crane planned a pilgrimage East to attend the American Unitarian Association Convention and the Women's Ministerial Conference and to visit historical sites in the Boston area. At the American Unitarian Association Conference she met the Reverend Minot J. Savage, whose writings and ministry she had admired for several years. His *Christianity: The Science of Manhood* was one of the most popular books among liberals in the West. Savage, minister of Unity Church of Boston, was one of the first American ministers to understand the religious possibilities of the theory of evolution.[34] After a conversation with Savage at the conference, Crane wrote in her diary: "Somehow I feel such an affection for Mr. Savage. I love the brave who are not harsh and unsympathetic. I hope to know him better though I will not intrude upon the attention of such a busy man."[35]

Impulsively, she went to hear him preach at his church a few days later, and for three days following the sermon she thought about writing him a letter. Finally she decided she must. Savage, in turn, invited her for a conference in his office, where they discussed at length the "Western Issue." He presented Crane with a copy of his new book, *The Morals of Evolution*.[36]

Another highlight of Crane's summer was a trip to Concord, Massachusetts, with the Reverend Grindall Reynolds, secretary and chief executive of the AUA, serving as her guide. Reynolds had met Crane in the fall of 1887 when he attended the dedication of the new Sioux Falls church.[37] For Crane, the trip was a visit to the home of her prophet, Ralph Waldo Emerson. Emerson, who had died in 1882, was initially a Unitarian minister who had studied at Harvard Divinity School, but his Romantic and mystical ideas differed greatly from the focus of contemporary Unitarian theology, which emphasized rationalism and science.

Reynolds and Emerson's devoted daughter, Ellen, who had remained at her father's side during his declining years, were close friends. After his death she continued to live at the poet's home. In her diary Crane remembered that she entered the house "in a trance." While she talked to Ellen, her mind was daydreaming about Emerson sitting at his old desk and speaking to her. On the desk was his pen, which for so many years had given the world his "matchless wisdom and sweetness," she wrote. Ellen invited Crane to be seated at her father's desk. Crane, still daydreaming, recalled the day that Emerson died and felt the poet's spirit was blessing her. Ellen led Reynolds and Crane to the library and then to the great old-fashioned garden where flowers were in bloom. As they left the house, Crane saw hanging on the wall the soft, gray felt garden hat that Emerson had worn. She felt strange. Was she imagining? Was there still in that piece of cloth a lingering suggestion of the philosopher's bodily expression? She touched the hat and fought back tears as Ellen cut and gave her all the flowers she could carry.

Crane took the flowers with her to Sleepy Hollow Cemetery. It was fitting, she thought, that Emerson's gravestone was a roughly-hewn boulder of rose granite that cast its shade over his grave. "The strength, the fineness, the gleaming purity, the matchless native beauty of that stone needs no external shape or polish—that is like Ralph Waldo Emerson," she wrote. The burial place was holy ground to her. She kissed the rock while tears streamed down her face. Crane said the tears "were grateful thanks for all he had inspired in her." Before leaving the cemetery, she placed the flowers on Emerson's grave, all but two violets, which she kept and pressed in her diary.

That summer Samuel J. Barrows, editor of the *Christian Register* and a member of the Harvard Divinity Class of 1875, invited Crane to attend the Harvard Divinity Alumni meeting in Divinity Hall. Crane was the only woman at the meeting, but Barrows, who was an advocate of a religion of civic righteousness, assured her she was welcome. Harvard maintained its sex discrimination policy, despite the fact that Meadville Seminary had allowed women into classes as early as 1868. The Harvard seminary had no direct denominational ties with the AUA but was managed by Unitarian ministers. The other primary seminary for Unitarian training was Manchester New College at Oxford, England, which also kept its doors closed to women. It distressed Crane that Unitarians were not the leaders in allowing women to study in their seminaries; Quakers and Universalists had been the most progressive denominations in accepting women.[38]

At the meeting Crane seized the opportunity to talk with several Harvard officials and alumni about the exclusion of women. The Reverend Samuel Longfellow, brother of the poet Henry Wadsworth Longfellow, and guest speaker Moncure D. Conway, a significant free thinker in London's Red Lion Square, seemed hospitable to the idea of admitting women, Crane wrote in her diary. Confessing to them with a little false humility that she did not believe herself to be the best specimen of womanhood in the pulpit, she tried to make them aware of some of the other important women ministers. The meeting was a great spectacle, an assembly of trained and cultured men ranging from graduates of half-century standing to youths who had just passed their examinations. There was a dark side to the gathering, Crane thought. It held but one woman minister, herself, and she was not really a part of the group, merely a guest of the day. Crane said in her diary that she had previously applied for admission to Harvard and been denied. She resented the exclusionary admittance policy that endured despite the existence of such world-recognized preachers as Julia Ward Howe and Mary Livermore. Also nearby was Boston University, a Methodist school and seminary, which admitted women to seminary and to medical college. Crane expressed her outrage that young men were actually recruited to attend Harvard's Divinity School. Scholarships were available to young men desiring to attend, while deserving young women could not gain admittance under any circumstance. Crane thought it ironic that there were committees of Unitarian women who toiled to raise money for scholarships to help educate promising young ministers. Someday, she thought, those men would preach to them from First Corinthians 14:34: "Let your women keep silent in the churches."[39]

In other events that summer, Crane participated in the Woman's Suffrage Festival in Boston and sat on the platform with suffrage leaders Lucy Stone, Julia Ward Howe, and Colonel Thomas Wentworth Higginson. She also attended a meeting of the Woman's Ministerial Conference, which Howe had founded, and gave a report there on women Unitarian ministers in Iowa and elsewhere.[40]

On July 27 she began her trip home. En route she stopped in Essex County, New York, and visited her father's birthplace. After a few days she boarded a train headed West through Canada. She looked out at the sun setting across Lake Champlain. It was so beautiful that she felt she must speak to someone about it. The only other passenger was a woman in the forward part of the coach who was looking out on the comparatively uninteresting landscape on the opposite side of the train. "I beg pardon, but you are missing such a glorious sunset," Crane said. The woman scarcely gave a glance in her direction and replied, "Oh, I live here."[41]

Crane's novitiate in the ministry was at an end. In a few weeks she would be in Kalamazoo, where her vision for improving her new community stretched far beyond the perception of most of the city's residents. She would see glorious possibilities where others scarcely cast a glance.

Crane assumed her pastorate at The First Unitarian Church of Kalamazoo on September 8, 1889, preaching before what she described as "a sea of wrinkled faces and gray hair." There were

7.

Unitarian minister Marion Murdock, left front, and Florence Buck, a
teacher, right front, pose with Caroline Bartlett, leaning on mantle, and
Stella Drake, a friend, at Caroline's apartment in Kalamazoo in the early
1890s.

only four children in the Sunday School that morning.[42] Since she immediately realized that the church needed more than a part-time ministry, Crane threw herself fully into the work of the church and postponed plans to attend theological classes in Chicago.[43]

Under her leadership the Sunday School and the Ladies Society were quickly reorganized, and church attendance as well as membership increased.[44] Crane's ordination was conducted on October 18 at the conclusion of the Michigan Unitarian Association annual convention, which was held at the Kalamazoo church. Among those participating in the ceremony were AUA Secretary Grindall Reynolds, William Channing Gannett, and Oscar Clute, who had inspired Crane to become a minister. Clute, who had been named president of the Michigan association by the conference, preached the ordination sermon. Crane's ordination ended her novitiate ministry, which she had served in Sioux Falls as an unordained sister minister.[45] The new responsibilities in Kalamazoo and her ordination were rites of passage. She no longer was known as "Carrie." "Carrie was more suitable for your little girl," she wrote her father. She said that in the future she would be known as "Caroline."[46] She had wedged herself into the world of men: she was a woman, not a girl, in charge.

Her responsibilities grew. In 1890, the Grand Rapids Unitarian congregation was without a minister, and Crane accepted an invitation to preach there every other Sunday. In response to this need, she asked the Kalamazoo congregation in the fall to name Iowa Sister Marion Murdock as Crane's co-pastor, an arrangement frequently adopted among the Iowa Sisterhood.[47]

Murdock and Crane resided in the same apartment, and Crane wrote her father and stepmother that under Murdock's influence she had given up coffee and tea and had become an

early riser. By late 1890, Crane decided to resign and travel in
Europe. Murdock, she thought, would be a perfect replacement,
despite her "chronic bronchial problems."[48] On January 12,
1891, Crane asked the church trustees to accept her resignation,
effective April 1.[49] Accompanied by a cousin—Miss Ada Brown
of Hawesville, Kentucky—Crane boarded a ship for England on
May 13.[50] She planned an extensive tour of Ireland, Scotland, and
England before going on to the European continent.

      In England, Crane became familiar with the work of
pioneer settlement houses and of the Salvation Army. In London
she visited Toynbee House,[51] the first settlement house, which was
an effort by university students to improve the cultural understanding and education of the poor,[52] and she met the superintendent
of the Charity Organization Society of London, which had been
founded in 1869. Soon afterwards, charity organizations were
being organized in the United States to centralize philanthropic
work. While settlement and charity work were important to her,
Crane was clearly more fascinated with the work of the Salvation
Army in London. She was introduced to its founder, General
William Booth, and met with other leaders of the organization,
including Captain Susan Swift, a native of Boston and graduate of
Vassar College. Its social work, not its evangelistic focus, attracted
Crane to the Salvation Army. "I went about a good deal with the
army to acquaint myself with the methods of appeal and to see the
type of people who were attracted by the brass bands and
hallujahs [sic] of the army," she said. Because of her ethical
liberal faith she was not allowed to speak at street meetings, but on
one occasion she was asked to pass the tambourine. Crane said
that at times the army members would meet with hostility. On
several occasions "sticks and decayed vegetables landed in our
midst, but I never knew anybody to really be hurt," she said.

Despite Crane's rejection of the evangelical and supernatural foundations of the Salvation Army's theology, she tried to fit in. "I always put off my good clothes for a black shawl and nondescript bonnet to look as much as possible like the other followers," she said.[53]

By the 1890s England was highly industrialized, and Crane was appalled at the social conditions of its cities. While in Manchester to preach, she viewed the workhouse at Crumstall and bemoaned the plight of the factory class whom she called "stunted forms" with "rounded shoulders." She wrote of her observations in a letter published in *Unity*, the magazine of the Western Unitarian Association:

> This is the penalty that England pays for generations of injustice to her working people: the physical and mental deterioration of a great mass of her inhabitants and countless workhouses and poor schools where vast numbers of incapables from the factory class are added to the numbers recruited from the usual sources of pauperism.[54]

During her tour of the workhouse Crane saw twelve dead workers who were "whitely swathed in their winding sheets." She added:

> It seemed to me these were happily out of a world that had no place for them, that so little knew its responsibility and so blithely held its way over these poor, stunted, starved ones that wearied and died unknowing, perhaps, what a world of human justice and brotherhood could have made for them.[55]

While she was in London she saw sights that she thought "ought not be in any city that calls itself civilized, much more Christian. The little boys laying on the cold pavement fast asleep."[56]

Entries in her diary, many of them very emotional, reveal that her excursions with the Salvation Army would have an impact on her later ministry. After spending a day in White Chapel and Drury Lane with Susan Swift, Crane wrote, "much that I saw would be too painful to describe—indeed words could not do justice to the woe and sin and misery of these regions in 'Darkest England'." Concerning the work of the Salvation Army members, she said: "Salvation Army women are saints and heroes if any there are in the world."[57]

During that summer Crane also learned about women's issues in England from members of the Women's Liberal League, which sought suffrage for women in parliamentary elections. To that time women taxpayers had been given the privilege of voting only in municipal elections. In London she was escorted to the House of Commons by a member of the league and was insulted by its gallery accommodations for women. Men had a spacious gallery from which to view debates, but women had only a twelve-by-five-foot box on the third floor, located above the speaker's chair in such a way that it was impossible to view his platform. Crane was incensed, also, that the women's gallery was enclosed by iron bars spaced so that she "could hardly put more than her fist through the spaces." She said she wanted to shake her fist through the bars at the members of Parliament. "What chance for parliamentary suffrage for women when men have the whole three sides of the second floor in an open gallery," she wrote in her diary of the summer.[58]

In England, Crane continued to search for opportunities for women to receive a theological education. She met with officials at Manchester New College in Oxford where male Unitarian and liberal ministers received their theological educations. She also brought up the question of the admission of women. In her diary, she said:

> . . . rather to my surprise, found the professors and trustees exceedingly interested, and really desirous that a test case should be made. They feel sure that it would be carried, and at least a dozen of the leading trustees and professors, including their legal adviser, say there isn't a word in the Constitution which could keep women out and promise their utmost help in case I can find any woman who will come.[59]

She showed them pictures of Murdock and Florence Buck of Kalamazoo, as well as about a dozen other women ministers. A year later Murdock and Buck did indeed study theology for a year at Manchester New College.[60] Crane found that many people in Great Britain thought she was the only woman preacher in the world until she produced her photographs of other woman ministers.[61]

　　She also journeyed to Morton, where she preached in the pulpit of the Reverend Philip Higginson, and her acquaintance with Higginson permitted her to meet his uncle, James Martineau, whom Crane greatly admired. She had been disappointed that Martineau, the foremost British Unitarian theologian, was not at his London home where she had planned to call on him. But Higginson forwarded a letter from Crane to Martineau at his summer home in northern Scotland. Crane took a train to Aviemore where—to her surprise—she was met at the station by the eighty-six-year-old theologian. He wanted to know more about women ministers in America. "How many women ministers are there in the United States?" he asked, and then wondered, "What were they like? Could they really preach? Do you think there would be more?" Fortunately, Crane had the photographs of women preachers she knew, including Julia Ward Howe, president of the Women's Ministerial Association, whose name was familiar to Martineau.[62]

In the meantime, Murdock, suddenly resigned two months after being named Crane's replacement in Kalamazoo. She had become close friends with Florence Buck, principal and head of the science department at Kalamazoo High School. Murdock announced that she would accompany Buck to the Meadville Seminary where Buck would begin her seminary education. Murdock would take post-graduate courses.[63] The church cabled Crane in London to ask her to return to Kalamazoo and resume her ministry. She accepted.[64]

A more confident Crane returned to Kalamazoo, and she immediately funneled social ideas from both her travels in Europe and the Western Unitarian ethical liberal position into her ministry. On April 10, 1892, she proposed a new church Bond of Union, which contained no references to Christianity and made "Truth, Righteousness, and Love" the only creedal tests for membership.[65] The bond borrowed its language and theology from the resolution offered at the 1886 Western Unitarian Conference, which had been written by the Reverend Gannett.[66] In addition, the church accepted a statement entitled "Things Most Commonly Believed Among Us," also adopted at the convention. The statement proclaimed that "to love Good and live the Good is the supreme thing in religion" and held that "reason and conscience," not creeds, were to be the final authorities in matters of religious belief. Unitarianism, it said, "is a religion of love to God and love to man."[67]

By the 1890s, Unitarians were more liberal in their interest in social issues than were their contemporaries. They believed that the church's focus was meant to be social and ethical.[68] Their ideas contributed to a new social awakening. Born during the Civil

War, the Social Gospel came to maturity during the Progressive Era prior to World War I. It was never an organized movement but a network of progressive ministers and churches operating within both the more conservative Protestant denominations such as the Baptists and the liberal Unitarians and Universalists.[69] Crane had been sympathetic to the concepts of the Social Gospel before she went to England, but after her return to the United States she renewed her dedication to a ministry that would bring the Kingdom of God to Kalamazoo. Most of the prominent advocates of the Social Gospel pastored churches in lower-class neighborhoods in big cities, but Crane believed that smaller cities such as Kalamazoo also had serious social problems.[70]

Crane was not alone in her new crusade. It was not unusual for Iowa sisters to develop extended family relationships with members of their churches,[71] and in Kalamazoo Crane had such a friendship with the Hubbard family. Her closest friend during this period was Caroline Hubbard,[72] and that friendship came to a special fruition when Crane announced that Silas Hubbard, Caroline Hubbard's father, had promised to give $20,000 toward the construction of a new church building. Under Crane's leadership the congregation had outgrown its old Gothic church building. Plans for a new church were made posthaste as Crane was named chairman of the building committee.[73] Hubbard said he was moved to make the donation because the church had influenced him to give up tobacco and alcohol, abstinence that saved him twice the amount of his gift to the church.[74] Hubbard's donation was conditional upon the inclusion of facilities for a kindergarten and an industrial school in the new building, requirements that were probably Crane's ideas. Like many of the Iowa sisters, she warmly embraced the kindergarten concept and G. Stanley Hall's developmental theories, which viewed childhood as a time to awaken the intellect with scientifically schooled parenting.[75] Immediately, the church embarked on a fund-raising project for the new church building. That autumn an architect was hired, but, as in Sioux Falls, it was Crane who actually designed the church.[76]

She laid a foundation for a new church philosophy as well. In a sermon Crane asked that the church become an unsectarian (non-denominational) "Creedless" church and change its name to "People's Church." Furthermore, she proposed that the church reorganize into an institutional "seven day church," similar to that of the Reverend Jenkin Lloyd Jones in Chicago.[77] She explained that this step would mean dropping the denominational Unitarian designation. "Unitarianism is dear to many of us," she said, but she felt that "People's Church" was a more proper name because it represented the needs and aspirations common to all men and women. Crane emphasized that Unitarianism in the West had discarded all creeds as fellowship tests, and she proposed that the denomination should logically complete its task by discarding the "theological test," Unitarianism, as well. She declared that the world now desired a church for humanity, not a church for theology. "Let us be that church, in our time and in our place, and what shall be the name for such but the 'People's Church'," she said. Crane clearly saw herself and the Kalamazoo church at the forefront of a new religious movement, although the church program and the name "People's Church" were not entirely original. She was familiar with the independent People's Church of Chicago and was a close associate with its pastor, the Reverend Hiram Thomas, who would give the address at the laying of the cornerstone.[78]

At a congregational meeting on April 23, 1893, the church approved the name change and the "seven day" program concept, as Crane warned that the action by the congregation to change the name might strain old ties of association.[79] Moreover, church records reveal no evidence that Crane or church leaders sought to withdraw from the Western Unitarian Conference. However, the church calendar and bulletin began to identify People's Church as "unsectarian"; nowhere on the monthly church calendars did the designation Unitarian appear.[80] Crane said the concept of the church and its programs would be modeled after

> an institutional seven day church of helpfulness that should know no bounds of race, or color or creed—a church where Trinitarians and Unitarians alike will find ever-open doors and hospitality to carry on any work that is for the help of the community; a church whose great aim shall be to help people as people, quite apart from their creed or no creed.[81]

The philosophy of the "seven day" church was the same as other products of the Social Gospel and Social Christianity: to adopt programs to improve the quality of life, and to focus on establishing the Kingdom of God on earth, instead of preparing the soul for eternal existence. By "institutional," Crane meant that the church would inaugurate social programs that the public sector—municipal and school government—had not yet had the foresight to initiate.[82] Crane believed that because the church had tax-exempt status it had a special duty to provide programs for the community, not just for its own members.[83]

The word "institutional" was used by several Social Gospelers to describe their social ministry.[84] Several ministers organized the "Open and Institutional Church League" in 1894 to agitate for enlarged church work in the cities. They hoped to bring about cities' social salvation through aggressive evangelistic, educational, and "institutional" programs. However, there is no evidence that Crane or People's Church joined this organization.

The new church was finished on schedule and dedicated the week of December 16, 1894. But the person responsible for the new building—Silas Hubbard—was not there; he had died in the fall.[85] The dedication involved former ministers, speeches by a host of outstanding Midwestern liberal and Unitarian ministers, banquets, and ceremonies. A Jewish rabbi and a Christian Science practitioner were among the speakers. During the dedication, the Michigan Unitarian Conference held its annual convention at the new church building, which did not look like a church to most visitors and residents. The next day, the Reverend Jenkin Lloyd Jones gave the dedicatory sermon urging the church to adopt a philosophy of progress in religion and social programs. As a symbolic gesture by the ministry of the church to "the people" of the community a banquet was given for the church's construction workers and their spouses on the evening before the dedicatory ceremony. More than 185 men and women attended the feast.[86]

The cost of the land and the new building was $35,000, but it was announced at the dedication that the building was debt-free, quite an accomplishment given the state of the national economy.[87] Money for the structure was raised during the so-called Panic of 1893, one of the serious depressions in American history. Despite the church's devotion to the building project, it still found time to lead charitable activities during the panic. During that winter, the church assisted the city by administering relief in one of the city's political wards.[88]

As in Sioux Falls, Crane created what was considered an unusual church building. Similar in design to other institutional churches, the structure lacked a lofty spire and so looked like a

8.

The exterior of People's Church constructed in 1894.

9.

The interior of People's Church in the 1890s.

college building, library, or hospital. The building's exterior was of red brick and stone. The auditorium seated five hundred, and at its front was a stage with a lectern; Crane would not have a pulpit in the church. The basement contained a dining area with sliding doors that opened into a room that was to be used for school and gymnasium.[89] The congregation revealed its enthusiasm for the new concept even before the church building was complete, by starting a public kindergarten, one of the first free public kindergarten classes in Michigan, as well as a vocational training school for men and boys.[90] The kindergarten opened in November of 1894 in the parlor and kitchen of the old church. The church offered the kindergarten program to the whole community. Crane loved the children, but she was especially devoted to working with parents. She met on a regular basis with mothers as well as fathers, and every two weeks conducted programs that allowed fathers to see what their children had done during the day.[91]

Shortly after the dedication ceremony a women's gymnasium program was started at the church. The program was made possible by the donation of equipment by Mrs. Silas Hubbard. A trained physical education director from the East was hired, and she had no trouble organizing day and evening classes for women and children. The gymnasium program was primarily for women because the city had an excellent YMCA for men.[92] Perhaps more noteworthy yet, however, was People's Church's commitment to working women. In the 1890s there were 150 small factories in the Kalamazoo area; many of which employed women. For several years the church offered inexpensive evening meals, mainly for these women.[93]

Though these programs on the home front occupied Crane's energies, she did have theological interests outside the local church. She attended state and national conventions but never showed any interest in Unitarian denominational leadership, probably because of her belief in a creedless church and her rejection of denominationalism. She was interested in the formation of the Congress of Liberal Religious Societies, which was inspired by the World Parliament of Religions held in 1893 in connection with the Chicago World's Fair.[94] Although he was not the recognized leader of the Parliament, the Reverend Jenkin Lloyd Jones was the guiding force behind it. The United States State Department invited three hundred national and foreign religious leaders, including several leaders of Eastern religions.

In addition to the World Parliament of Religions, Crane attended several other events at the World's Fair, and served as a delegate to the Woman's Congress of Representative Women, which met at the fair's Woman's Building. She also served as chairwoman of one of the Sunday sessions.[95] The Chicago World's Fair, held along the Lake Michigan shore, was one of the few cheery aspects of life in 1893 as the nation suffered from a depression. Newspapers reported that 25,000 people in Chicago were without a place to sleep.[96]

Everyone who could afford it went to the fair's Columbia Exposition, which marked the four-hundredth anniversary of the discovery of the New World. Crane made her own discovery at the fair. She found that the tyranny of women's clothing restricted her ability to enjoy the event. After a few days, she tired of picking up the hem of her dress to maneuver through mud and dirt, and she cut seven inches off her skirt, making it fall to a point above her ankles. This attracted the stares and indignation of other fairgoers, and the first morning after her tailoring breakthrough, the streetcar conductor was reluctant to let her ride. "Here is my adult ticket," she said to him, who most likely had seen such shortened shirts worn only by young girls.[97] Crane not only displayed her courage on distant shores but also modeled the dress for her women's club in Kalamazoo.[98]

It was with a mind more on justice than on fashion that Crane approached the first national meeting of the National Congress of Liberal Religious Societies in 1894, which was under the leadership of the Reverend Hiram Thomas. It was attended by an independent (Thomas), twenty-eight rabbis, seventy Unitarian ministers, twelve Universalist ministers, and four Ethical Culture leaders.[99] It convened at Sinai Temple in Chicago on May 22 with Crane as the primary speaker on women's issues. In her speech, she condemned the divisions between the sexes and urged the congress to oppose prejudices based on sex. It was hoped that the congress would encourage the organization of nondenominational churches that allowed absolute freedom of religious belief.[100] Crane was a national director of the organization and an associate editor of *New Unity*, the official publication of the congress.[101] The Reverend Jenkin Lloyd Jones was editor of the publication and general secretary of the Congress.

Crane saw her church as part of an institutional church movement that was inspired by this congress and by the Parliament of Religions. In an interview she said:

> The institutional church, undenominational and non-sectarian, is a movement growing out of the scientific spirit of the day on the one hand and the humanitarian spirit on the other. This spirit found its best expression in the congress of religions held in Dr. Hirsch's church (Sinai Temple) last spring, and that in turn was the child of the parliament of religions. It looks toward a union of the liberal forces on a practical rather than a theological basis. There are very few institutional churches in the country, and of these the new church in Kalamazoo is the only one known to me that is

nonsectarian and without any creedal requirements for
membership. My new church will be absolutely free from any
denominational test. There are a number of evangelical
churches having "institutional" features, but most of them
require subscription to some creed on the ground of
membership.[102]

In spite of its bright beginnings, the congress had little success as a
new religious organization. By the turn of the century it had been
dissolved due to the withdrawal of Jewish support and the un-
willingness of Unitarian churches to affiliate with it and support it
fully. Both Jewish groups and Unitarian churches saw the
Congress as a new denomination and would not forego their
previous allegiances.[103]

The general focus of Crane's seven-day ministry was civic,
social, and political reform, but she was particularly interested in
the contributions women could make toward improving society.
During the early years of the suffrage struggle women had
claimed they were equal to men and thus had a natural right to
political equality, but when this argument was not well received
many women, in frustration, turned to municipal suffrage as an
interim alternative.[104] To some extent, municipal suffrage was an
outgrowth of the concept of municipal housekeeping, a philosophical basis for social action that was first institutionalized as early as
the 1870s by women's clubs in Boston, Buffalo, and New York
City.[105] Building on their skills as managers of their own
households, women, it was believed, could extend their concerns to
the municipalities in which they lived, and, were they able to vote
in local elections, they would be even more effective in dealing
with the problems of the cities. Crane had argued early in her
ministry in Kalamazoo that municipal affairs were not too
complicated for women to understand, that the city was, in effect,

simply a group of homes, and that the sanitary precautions a city must take were similar to those involved in house cleaning, if on a larger scale.[106] Women, she felt, were especially capable of being municipal housekeepers.

In Michigan women began their battle for municipal suffrage in the state legislature in 1883, arguing that it was a natural extension of a woman's concern for the health and safety of her family. The following year women suffragists formed the Michigan Equal Suffrage Association (MESA), and for the next decade its primary goal was to obtain the vote for women in city elections.[107] The Women's Christian Temperance Union and the women's clubs of Michigan joined in the struggle. Crane was a member of the Kalamazoo chapter of the WCTU and the Twentieth Century Club, which in 1893 became affiliated with the General Federation of Women's Clubs. The local club had been founded by Lucinda Hinsdale Stone of Kalamazoo, who for her efforts in forming women's clubs throughout the state was known as the "Mother of Michigan Clubs."[108] Stone and her husband, James, former president of Kalamazoo College, had been instrumental in opening the University of Michigan to women.

Soon after her arrival in Kalamazoo, Crane became a board member of the Michigan Equal Suffrage Association. She attended the National American Woman Suffrage Association convention in Washington, D.C., in 1891 and delivered the closing sermon.[109] NAWSA was still a small organization at this time, with only thirteen thousand members, compared to a membership of twenty thousand in the GFWC, which had been founded only a year earlier, and 200,000 in the WCTU.[110] MESA's efforts to gain municipal suffrage culminated in 1893. That year the legislature heard speeches by NAWSA leaders Susan B. Anthony and Anna Howard Shaw as well as by Crane. On first consideration, the municipal suffrage bill was defeated in the House by a 38–39 vote, but before the session adjourned in May the bill was reconsidered and passed by a 57–25 margin. The Senate joined in passing the bill, 18–11, and it was signed into law by the governor.[111] Election officials in Detroit challenged the new law, and on October 24, 1893, the State Supreme Court ruled it unconstitutional. The legislature, the court said, had no right to create a new class of voters.[112]

But Crane did not give up hope. Michigan women planned new strategies at MESA's annual meeting in January 1894,[113] which included lectures by Anthony, Shaw, and Crane. Later, Michigan suffragists sought complete enfranchisement through statewide referendum and constitutional amendment. Although MESA did forego the concept of municipal suffrage after 1893, Crane continued to believe that it was an expedient solution.

In 1896, Crane was a speaker at the Biennial Convention of the General Federation of Women's Clubs in Louisville, Kentucky.[114] There she also lectured to the local Women's Christian Temperance Union. The WCTU maintained that if women had the vote, they would purify society and clean up a political system corrupted by big liquor interests. Crane urged the Louisville WCTU to support municipal suffrage for women because the vote would make them more effective housekeepers. She said, in part:

> Let us take the sphere of municipal politics—the department to which women have naturally turned. What is a municipality but an aggregation of households? Lighting, sanitation, the city house cleaning, all the things which pertain to the building up of the city are the same problems which women

have to grasp to a lesser degree in their households. The facts
are that every one of these pursuits appeal more vitally to
women than to men because they touch the home.[115]

Crane also was interested in such social issues as the death
penalty and assistance to the poor. She went to the Michigan state
capital in 1892 to lobby against a bill authorizing the death
penalty in Michigan, and she preached from her pulpit about the
need for prison reform. "Capital punishment does not decrease
crime, and it is against the dictates of humanity," she said in a
sermon. In another sermon she urged special rehabilitation efforts
for first-time criminal offenders.[116] From her lectern at People's
Church she reported that at least three hundred men in Kalamazoo
were without work, and she urged city government to find
employment for them through public works projects. She
preached that it was the church's "duty to the poor" to support
government that provided jobs for the poor, instead of providing
indiscriminate relief. "The county votes a sum for the needy who
are not in any of its institutions, and it is given without any
return," she said; and "we must support the aged, infirm,
incompetent and sometimes the wife and children, but the
able-bodied man or woman should be obliged, forced, to furnish
his or her own support in one way or another."[117]

Crane's position as a minister provided her with the
opportunity to provide leadership in social reform activities in
Kalamazoo. She became convinced that the official responsible
for the distribution of poor funds in Kalamazoo County was
heartless and treated the poor cruelly. In January 1896 she
initiated an attempt to oust the county's poormaster from office.
For sixteen years Henry W. Bush had dispensed moneys for poor
relief, which in 1895 totaled $20,000 annually. Crane appeared
before the County Board of Supervisors and charged that Bush

was "harsh, cruel, and profane" in his dispensing of the poor aid. She asked that he be dismissed from office for incompetence. At a hearing on the issue Crane was denounced by Bush's attorney as a "meddler, a disturber of the peace, and a woman seeking notoriety by persecuting an old man who had faithfully served the county for years." A total of nineteen witnesses appeared against Bush, testifying that he had refused to provide aid and claiming that he had called applicants "lazy Dutch loafer," "niggers," and "little black cusses." In addition, allegations were made that he received kickbacks from a local undertaker and a wood merchant. The twenty-one member board found Bush guilty of incompetence in office, using cruel and harsh language, and denying aid to those who deserved it. He was fired and replaced. But Bush refused to surrender his position, and his attorney appealed to the Circuit Court judge for a review of the proceedings. The court later reinstated Bush, saying that the poor-master had not been properly notified of the charges and that they were not specific enough.[118]

The plight of the poor occupied only one portion of Crane's interest. As an Iowa sister, the teaching role was important to her, and the main conduit for that activity was the Unity Club, which had about one hundred members in Kalamazoo. Although sponsored by the church, the Unity Club claimed to be independent of church control. Literature, comparative religion, politics, history, and the new social science of sociology were among the favored topics. The name *Unity Club* and the club's concept were coined in Humboldt, Iowa, by Sister Mary Safford.[119] The development of sociology during the last two decades of the nineteenth century provided secular reinforcement to the theology of secular activism. In the fall of 1896 the social science division of the church's Unity Club embarked upon its most impressive project—preparation of a sociological survey the city. The work was entitled "A Study of the Social Conditions of Kalamazoo." Members of the club were assigned topics and gave reports at regular meetings. For example, the question "How is the City Nourished?" called for research on the sources, distribution, and consumption of supplies. The topic "How Does the City Protect Itself?" called for research on fire, police, and health services. Also addressed were waste disposal, water supply, the geology and typography of the city, social classes and conditions, schools, colleges, and churches.[120] The study was done "in consultation" with the Department of Sociology at the University of Chicago, but it was more than a fact-collecting exercise. According to the People's Church calendar, "The object is not merely to obtain information, but information of a kind that will lead to more rational methods in endeavoring to improve the sociological condition of our city."[121] Completed in the spring of 1897, the study was submitted to University of Chicago sociology professor Charles Henderson, who critiqued it and forwarded the research documents to other cities seeking information on how to conduct scientific social studies.

The chief purpose of sociology was to find out the truth about society and to create programs that would ameliorate its social woes. The fathers of sociology believed that the real value of sociology as pure science would be its use as an index and a text to measure what is worth doing in the world. The Social Gospelers as "doers" were supportive of sociology because it provided a scientific foundation for their belief that the church's main purpose was to create a better and more ethical society.[122] Although she saw the science of sociology as a Christian course of study, Crane was less enthusiastic about socialism. She attacked the excesses of capitalism in an 1896 sermon, but she never advocated socialism as a solution to social problems.[123]

Crane's efforts toward sociological improvement were varied. As her kindergarten program illustrated, she believed that she could play an important role in the education of children. An Audubon Society for children was formed at the church, and Crane published a year-long Sunday School course on "Good Citizenship" for children. She also promoted educational opportunities for blacks in the community, creating a literary club at the church.[124] A year after its founding, the Frederick Douglass Club moved its meetings from People's Church to black churches in the community. Blacks also were welcome at her church services, and a few attended on occasion.

Meanwhile, during the winter of 1896, People's Church was highly publicized, and Crane became a national celebrity. On January, 10, 1896, Colonel Robert Ingersoll, "the Great Agnostic," spoke in Kalamazoo. The archenemy of conservative evangelicals, Ingersoll contended that he was not an atheist but an agnostic—one who simply did not know whether God exists. He had recently survived a prayer vigil held in his honor by thousands of members of The Christian Endeavor Society in Cleveland and other cities, who asked God for Ingersoll's conversion.[125] Ingersoll had arrived in Kalamazoo on Friday afternoon, January 9, for an evening speech on Abraham Lincoln. Crane asked Mayor Otto Ihling to see whether he could arrange for her to meet Ingersoll. The mayor was successful, and after formalities, Ingersoll asked Bartlett: "Well, what is your little 'ism'?"[126] In response to his remark, she said she would like to give him a tour of People's Church and explain its programs. At first he refused, but finally he was persuaded by the persistent Crane, who said after the tour, "I believe in God and immortality and prayer, but I grant perfect freedom to every member of the church to believe what is believable to him. If I could stand your prayerlessness, Colonel Ingersoll, could you stand my prayer?" Ingersoll stated:

> Yes, if all churches were like this—free, always open and working to make people better every day—I would never say one word against churches or religion. If I lived here I would join this church, if it would receive me.

That night Ingersoll told his Kalamazoo audience of his visit to the People's Church and said: "It is the grandest thing in your state, if not the United States. If there were a similar church near my home, I would join it, if its members would permit me."[127] The news dispatch reporting Ingersoll's comment was interpreted by the Christian Endeavors as evidence that Ingersoll had been converted. But orthodox clamor was soon silenced when the press explained that the People's Church was considered by Kalamazoo's orthodox churchmen to be heretical and almost atheistic. The story made the front page in newspapers in such major cities as New York, Boston, and Chicago.[128] Alongside an article in the *New York Journal* were telegraph messages from Crane and Ingersoll, who by then was in Toledo.[129] In his response, Ingersoll avoided affirming or denying reports concerning the precise nature of his comments. He briefly outlined the social work of the church and explained its creedlessness. He then concluded his remarks by saying "Miss Bartlett . . . is a remarkable person. She has intelligence of the highest order, great industry and that divine thing called enthusiasm. I like that church."[130] On January 24, 1896, apparently in response to a note from Crane, Ingersoll wrote to her:

It was not necessary for you to tell me that you had nothing to
do with the report that went from Kalamazoo. I know all about
papers and reporters. I was not annoyed. On the contrary, I
was gratified. I hope that I did no injury and if I did you the
least good, I am more than gratified. I respect and admire you
and take a real interest in your work.[131]

On Sunday, January, 19, 1896, Crane spoke before an
overflow crowd at People's Church on the topic: "Why People's
Church Should Fellowship Col. Ingersoll?" She admitted her
religious beliefs were far from Ingersoll's but said she supported
his beliefs more than those of his critics, the evangelicals. She
pointed out that the principle of fellowship at People's Church
was the conviction that the things that "divide well-meaning
people are superficial, while the things which unite them are
fundamental." Ingersoll has been maligned and misrepresented,
she said, "because he condemns only the false and cruel theology
of a god of cruelty as revealed in portions of the Old Testament."[132] Although the incident probably was of no benefit to
Ingersoll, it provided Crane with a forum for publicizing her
ministry. In her statements to the press she explained that People's
Church had a fellowship wide enough to embrace all who wished
to be good and do good—liberal, evangelical, Catholic, Jew,
agnostic, Christian Scientist, or spiritualist. She said that the
current church membership included members from all those
faiths, except Catholics, "and the church's relationships with
Roman Catholics was cordial."[133] Crane even encouraged contact
with the occult and Eastern religions. After her return from
Europe in 1891, she taught a course on Eastern religions at
People's Church. One of the lectures was titled "Buddha, the
Hindu Christ."[134] Spiritualists had attended People's Church
services and were allowed to use People's Church for their

services. Crane attended seances but said she was not convinced of the ability of a medium to reach a supernatural world.[135]

People's Church continued to become a larger force in the community. Christians in conservative Kalamazoo called many of her projects heretical, even boycotting her effort to organize a Christmas community-wide benefit for the poor.[136] Crane had defined a social and humanitarian mission for People's Church and it had grown. It was not uncommon for three or four hundred people to attend services, quite a remarkable accomplishment for a liberal church viewed with suspicion by many people.

But the height of her work and success, Crane drastically changed her way of life. On August 17, 1896, she celebrated her thirty-eighth birthday. Like many of the Iowa Sisters, she had remained unmarried because she believed domestic responsibilities would hinder her professional career. Caroline had been seriously courted by Augustus Warren Crane, a physician, who had opened a general practice in Kalamazoo shortly after his graduation as valedictorian of the University of Michigan medical class of 1894. The leader of the young men's Sunday School class at People's Church, Warren, as Caroline called him, was ten years younger than she. The age difference caused eyebrows in the community to arch,[137] and letters written by Warren to Caroline indicate they had a stormy courtship. Caroline, it seems, was reluctant to become romantically involved. "Never once had we accepted each other without reservations whatsoever," he wrote. "Yet I have loved you without reservations."[138] He recalled in one of the letters that she had said that "the thought of being his wife has never given me any pleasure." But, despite her reluctance, they were married on New Year's Eve, 1896, in a wedding ceremony that proved to be a mild practical joke on all but a few of their close friends.

At the previous Sunday service, Crane had told her congregation that because they had given her several receptions, she wished to return the courtesy by giving a congregational reception at the church on New Year's Eve. At about nine o'clock, a musical program started and guests assembled in the church auditorium. Meanwhile, Crane was hurriedly driven to her apartment, where she donned her wedding gown. At the close of the musical program the Reverend Jenkin Lloyd Jones came to the pulpit and announced that Caroline was to be married. The buzz from the audience was nearly as loud as the initial chords of "Angel's Serenade" played by the organist to start the ceremony.

Warren walked briskly down the right aisle, and Caroline walked at a slower, sedate pace down the left. Jones stood waiting; the bride and groom were both unattended. After reading vows that each had composed, Jones pronounced their marriage, and they received his blessing with bowed heads and clasped hands. The surprised audience congratulated the couple at a reception following the ceremony. A dinner party was given for them on New Year's Day, and they both returned to work the next day, without a wedding trip.[139]

NOTES

[1]Crane, "The Story and the Results," p. 11.

[2]Crane, "The Story and the Results," p. 11.

[3]Sydney E. Ahlstrom, *A Religious History of the American People* (New Haven and London: Yale University Press, 1972), p. 779.

[4]Caroline Bartlett to Oscar Clute, 8 October 1886, Crane Papers, Western Michigan University Archives.

[5]Department of the Interior, Bureau of Census, *Eleventh Census of the United States, 1890: Population* 2: ci. (According to the report, there were sixty-seven women ministers in 1870, 165 in 1880, and 1,143 in 1890.)

[6]Program of the Iowa Unitarian Association Conference, 1886, Crane Papers.

[7]Catherine Hitchings, *Universalist and Unitarian Women Ministers* (Boston: Universalist Historical Society, 1975), pp. 4–5; and Charles H. Lyttle, *Freedom Moves West: A History of the Western Unitarian Conference 1852–1952* (Boston: Beacon Press, 1952), pp. 146–47.

[8]Hitchings, *Universalist and Unitarian Women Ministers*, p. 109.

[9]"The Unitarian Home," unidentified Sioux Falls newspaper, undated, Nell Hudson Scrapbooks, Crane Papers.

[10]Cynthia Grant Tucker, *A Woman's Ministry: Mary Collson's Search for Reform as a Unitarian Minister, a Hull House Social Worker, and a Christian Science Practitioner* (Philadelphia: Temple University Press, 1984), p. 9; and Hitchings, *Universalist and Unitarian Woman Ministers*, p. 129.

[11]"The Unitarian Home," Nell Hudson Scrapbooks.

[12]"The Unitarian Home," Nell Hudson Scrapbooks.

[13]"The Unitarian Home," Nell Hudson Scrapbooks.

[14]"The Unitarian Home," Nell Hudson Scrapbooks.

[15]Charles Howard Hopkins, *The Rise of the Social Gospel in American Protestantism 1865–1915* (New Haven: Yale University Press, 1940), p. 318.

[16]*The Rise of the Social Gospel*, p. 320.

[17]Caroline J. Bartlett, *Natural or Revealed Religion*, a sermon delivered 21 October 1888, Sioux Falls, Dakota Territory (Yankton, Dakota Territory: Press and Dakotaian Print, 1888), p. 6, Crane Papers; Frederick Ives Carpenter, *Emerson Handbook* (New York: Hendricks House, 1953), pp. 108–35; and Ralph Waldo Emerson, "The Transcendentalist," *Selected Writings of Emerson,* ed. Donald McQuade (New York: Modern Library, 1981), p. 20.

[18]Caroline J. Bartlett, *Natural or Revealed Religion*, p. 5.

[19]Bartlett, *Natural or Revealed Religion*, p. 7; and Hopkins, *The Rise of the Social Gospel,* p. 123.

[20]Caroline J. Bartlett, *The Sacredness of Present Time,* 1 September 1889, publisher unknown in Sioux Falls, Dakota Territory, Crane Papers.

[21]Charles H. Lyttle, *Freedom Moves West*, pp. 163–92.

[22]Lyttle, *Freedom Moves West*, p. 148

[23]Caroline J. Bartlett, *Creeds: Their Use and Abuse,* a sermon given 25 September 1887, at the All Souls Church, Sioux Falls, Dakota Territory (Sioux Falls, Dakota Territory: All Souls Unitarian Church, 1887), Crane Papers.

[24]C. H. Cramer, *Royal Bob: The Life of Robert G. Ingersoll* (Indianapolis: Bobbs-Merrill Co., 1952), p. 55; and Caroline J. Bartlett, *Truths and Errors in Col. Ingersoll's Method and Argument,* a speech delivered at Sioux Falls, Dakota Territory, 16 December, 1888, and published by All Souls Unitarian Church, Sioux Falls, pp. 3–5, Crane Papers.

[25]"Once a Reporter," *Minneapolis Tribune* (25 May 1889), Crane Papers.

26Caroline J. Bartlett to Lorenzo and Louise Bartlett, 18 November 1891, Crane Papers.

27Lyttle, *Freedom Moves West*, p. 186; and Oscar Clute to Caroline Bartlett, 23 May 1887, Crane Papers.

28"Dedication," undated newspaper clipping, Nell Hudson Scrapbooks.

29Caroline Bartlett Crane, "People's Church," 1934 typescript recollections, p. 4, Crane Papers.

30Caroline Bartlett Crane, "The Story and the Results," p. 13; Secretary of State, *Census of the State of Michigan, 1884*, 1:500.

31Caroline Bartlett Crane, "People's Church," p. 4.

32"A Gifted Lady," *Kalamazoo Daily Telegraph* (17 March 1889; Microfilm Reproduction, University Microfilms: Ann Arbor, Michigan, and available in the Western Michigan University Archives and Regional History Collections, Kalamazoo, Michigan).

33Church Minutes, Board of Trustees, People's Church Library Archives, Kalamazoo, Michigan.

34Samuel Atkins Eliot, ed., *The Pilots: Heralds of a Liberal Faith Series*, vol. 4 (Boston: The Beacon Press, 1952), p. 169.

35Caroline J. Bartlett, "Diary of Summer of 1889," no page numbers, Crane Papers.

36Caroline J. Bartlett, "Diary of Summer of 1889."

37Bartlett, "Dairy of Summer of 1889."

38Caroline Bartlett, "The Liberal Minister: His Equipment and Place," First Unitarian Church of Kalamazoo, 1892, Kalamazoo, Michigant, Crane Papers; and Hitchings, *Universalists and Unitarian Women Ministers,* pp. 4–5.

[39]Bartlett, "Diary of Summer of 1889."

[40]Caroline Bartlett, "The Liberal Minister: His Equipment and Place."

[41]Caroline Bartlett Crane, "My Father," p. 1.

[42]Caroline Bartlett Crane, "The Story of an Institutional Church in a Small City," *Charities and the Commons* 14 (May 6, 1905): 723–31.

[43]"History of the First Unitarian Church of Kalamazoo, 1858–1894," People's Church Library Archives; and Caroline Bartlett to Lorenzo and Louise Bartlett, 16 September 1889, Crane Papers.

[44]Records of the church clerk, People's Church, Kalamazoo, Michigan, as reported in the Minutes of the Board of Trustees, 13 January 1890, People's Church Library Archives.

[45]Crane, "The Story and the Results," p. 12; program for the ordination of Caroline J. Bartlett, 18 October 1889, Crane Papers; "Ordination," *Kalamazoo Daily Telegraph* (19 October 1889; Microfilm Reproduction, University Microfilms: Ann Arbor, Michigan, in Western Michigan University Archives); and "The First One Hundred Years: Michigan State College," a pamphlet published by Michigan State College, East Lansing, Michigan, 1955, n. 9.

[46]Caroline J. Bartlett to Lorenzo Bartlett, September 1889, Crane Papers.

[47]"History of the First Unitarian Church of Kalamazoo, 1858–1894"; and Church Minutes, Board of Trustees, 12 January 1891, People's Church Library Archives.

[48]Caroline J. Bartlett to Louise Bartlett, 22 September 1890; and Caroline J. Bartlett to Lorenzo and Louise Bartlett, 6 October 1890, Crane Papers.

[49]Church Minutes, Board of Trustees, 12 January 1891, People's Church Library Archives.

[50]"History of the First Unitarian Church of Kalamazoo, 1858–1894"; and "Farewell Reception," undated newspaper clipping, Nell Hudson Scrapbooks, Crane Papers.

[51]Ibid.

[52]Allen F. Davis, *Spearheads for Reform: The Social Settlements and the Progressive Movement 1890–1914* (New York: Oxford University Press, 1967), p. 3.

[53]Caroline Bartlett Crane, "Salvation Army," 1934 typescript recollections, Crane Papers.

[54]Caroline Bartlett Crane, "English Letter," *Unity* (23 July 1891) pp. 179–80.

[55] Crane, "English Letter," *Unity* (23 July 1891) pp. 179–80.

[56]Crane, "1891 Europe Diary," vol. 2, p. 60, Crane Papers.

[57]Crane, "1891 Europe Diary, " vol. 2, p. 76.

[58]Crane, "1891 Europe Diary," vol. 2, pp. 54–58.

[59]Crane, "1891 Europe Diary," vol. 3, p. 33.

[60]"Kalamazoo Honored," unidentified Kalamazoo newspaper, undated, Crane Papers. (The clipping says that Buck and Murdock had been asked to take the co-pastorate of the Unity Church in Cleveland, Ohio. At the time of the announcement they were studying at Manchester New College where Bartlett's effort made it possible for them to become the first women admitted to theological courses); and "Women in the Pulpit," *New York Telegram*, undated, Nell Hudson Scrapbooks, Crane Papers.

[61]Michigan Authors Association, *Proceedings of Michigan Authors Association*, by Caroline Bartlett Crane, Benton Harbor, Michigan, 12 May 1928, p. 27; and Crane, "1891 Europe Diary," vol. 5.

[62]Crane, "1891 Europe Dairy;" and Caroline Bartlett, "English Letter," *Unity* (23 July 1891): 179–80.

[63]Hitchings, *Universalist and Unitarian Women Ministers*, pp. 35, 109.

[64]Church Minutes, Board of Trustees, 10 April 1892, People's Church Library Archives.

[65]"History of First Unitarian Church of Kalamazoo," section designated 1891–92. (Copies of "Bond of Union" and "Things Most Commonly Believed Among Us"); and Church Minutes, Board of Trustees, 10 April 1892, People's Church Library Archives; Church Minutes, Board of Trustees, 17 April 1892, People's Church Library Archives.

[66]Lyttle, *Freedom Moves West,* pp. 182–85, 189.

[67]"History of First Unitarian Church of Kalamazoo," section designated 1891–92.

[68] Hopkins, *The Rise of the Social Gospel*, pp. 3–4.

[69]Hopkins, *The Rise of the Social Gospel*, p. 320.

[70]Crane, "The Story of an Institutional Church," p. 723.

[71]Cynthia Grant Tucker, *Prophetic Sisterhood: Liberal Women Ministers of the Frontier, 1880–1930* (Boston: Beacon Press, 1990), p. 74.

[72]Caroline Bartlett Crane, "The Life of Caroline Kleinstuck," unpublished typescript ca. 1933, Crane Papers. (The typescript manuscript provides biographical data about Caroline Hubbard Kleinstuck and her father, Silas, and insight into Caroline's relationship with the Hubbard family); and "A Gift of Humanity," unidentified Kalamazoo newspaper, undated, Nell Hudson Scrapbooks, Crane Papers.

[73]Church Minutes, Board of Trustees, 20 February and 10 March 1893, People's Church Library Archives.

[74]Church Minutes, Board of Trustees, 10 March 1893, People's Church Library Archives.

[75]Tucker, *Prophetic Sisterhood,* p. 94.

[76]Church Minutes, Board of Trustees, 25 June 1894, People's Church Library Archives; and "People's Church—Name Stone Placed," *Kalamazoo Daily News* (26 June 1894), Crane Papers.

[77]"People's Church—Still More Liberal," *Kalamazoo Daily News* 24 April 1894, Crane Papers.

[78]"People's Church—Name Stone Placed," *Kalamazoo Daily News,* 26 June 1894, Crane Papers, Western Michigan University Archives.

[79]Church Minutes, Board of Trustees, 23 April 1894, People's Church Library Archives.

[80]All the published church calendars from 1895 to 1898 indicate on the front cover that the church is "unsectarian." Church calendars are available in the Crane Papers and in the People's Church Library Archives.

[81]Crane, "The Story of an Institutional Church," p. 731.

[82]Crane, "The Story of the Institutional Church," p. 731.

[83]Caroline Bartlett Crane, "Biographical Sketch," p. 2, Crane Papers.

[84]Hopkins, *The Rise of the Social Gospel,* p. 154.

[85]"Silas Hubbard," *Kalamazoo Daily News* (10 September 1894), Crane Papers.

[86]"Is Dedicated," *Kalamazoo Daily Telegraph* (20 December 1894), Crane Papers.

[87]"Free of Debt," unidentified Kalamazoo newspaper, undated, Crane Papers.

[88]Crane, "The Story of an Institutional Church," p. 730.

[89]"Free of Debt," Crane Papers; and "Memoir Silas Hubbard, 1812–1894," pamphlet published by the congregation of People's Church (1 March 1896, p. 35), Crane Papers.

[90]Crane, "The Story of an Institutional Church," p. 728.

[91]Crane, "The Story of an Institutional Church," p. 724.

[92]Crane, "The Story of an Institutional Church," p. 728.

[93]Helen Christine Bennett, "Caroline Bartlett Crane of Kalamazoo: The First Municipal Expert of America," *Pictorial Review* (September 1910) p. 13; and Caroline Bartlett Crane; "Biographical Sketch," p. 17, Crane Papers.

[94]Lyttle, *Freedom Moves West,* p. 25.

[95]Program of Woman's Congress of Representative Women. (Bartlett wrote on the program that she conducted a Sunday morning session, substituting for suffragist Anna Howard Shaw.) Crane Papers.

[96]Harold Underwood Faulkner, *Politics, Reform and Expansion 1890–1900* (New York: Harper and Brothers, 1959), p. 163.

[97]Crane, "Method of Dress, Then and Now," 1934 typescript recollections, pp. 1–2.

[98]"How to See It; Miss Bartlett Tells About the Great Show," unidentified Kalamazoo newspaper, undated, Crane Papers.

[99]Lyttle, *Freedom Moves West,* p. 205.

[100]Congress of Liberal Religious Societies, *Official Report of the Proceedings of the First American Congress of Liberal Religious Societies,* "What Women Can Do in Uniting the Cultural and Religious Forces of Society," by Caroline J. Bartlett (Chicago: Bloch & Newman, 1894), pp. 18–21, Crane Papers.

[101]The masthead of *New Unity,* new series 3 (6 August 1896): 389, Crane Papers.

[102]"New Church in Kalamazoo," unidentified Kalamazoo newspaper, undated, Nell Hudson Scrapbooks, Crane Papers.

[103]C. H. Cramer, *Royal Bob: The Life of Robert G. Ingersoll,* p. 161.

[104]Aileen S. Kraditor, *The Ideas of the Woman Suffrage Movement, 1890–1920* (New York: Columbia University Press, 1965).

[105]Karen J. Blair, *The Clubwoman as Feminist,* pp. 73–74.

[106]"Duties for Citizenship," unidentified Kalamazoo newspaper, undated, Nell Hudson Scrapbooks, Crane Papers.

[107]Virginia Ann Paganelli Caruso, "A History of Woman Suffrage in Michigan, " (Ph.D. diss., Michigan State University, 1986), pp. 90–104.

[108]Mary M. Lewis Hoyt, *Woman's Forum* (Kalamazoo: Women's Federated Clubs, 1932), p. 30.

[109]Susan B. Anthony and Ida Husted Harper, eds., *The History of Woman Suffrage*, vol. 4 (Rochester, N.Y.: Source Book Press, Susan B. Anthony, 1902), p. 184. (*The History of Woman Suffrage* is composed of six volumes. Several editors were involved in the compilation of the series over a period of years. The first three volumes, which cover the years prior to 1890, were edited by Elizabeth Cady Stanton, Susan B. Anthony, and Matilda Joslyn Gage. The first two were published in 1881, in Rochester, New York, and the third in 1886. Volume 4 was edited by Anthony and Harper and was published in 1902 in Rochester. Harper also edited the fifth and sixth volumes, which were published in 1922 in New York by the NAWSA.)

[110]Ruth Bordin, *Woman and Temperance* (Philadelphia: Temple University Press, 1981), p. 3. The figure for NAWSA may be found in the *Proceedings of the Twenty-Fifth Annual Convention of the National American Woman Suffrage Association, held in Washington, D.C., January 16–19, 1893,* p. 16, as cited in Aileen S. Kraditor in the *Ideas of the Woman Suffrage Movement*, p. 7.

[111]Caruso, "A History of Woman Suffrage in Michigan," pp. 104–09; Anthony and Harper; *The History of Woman Suffrage,* vol. 4, p. 764; Michigan State Legislature, "An Act to Secure to Women Citizens Who are Otherwise Qualified

the Right to Vote in School, Village, and City Elections," in *Public Acts, 1893, Regular Session*, Act 138, pp. 225–26.

112Caruso, "A History of Woman Suffrage in Michigan," pp. 118–19.

113Michigan Equal Suffrage Association, *Proceedings of the Annual Convention of the Michigan Equal Suffrage Association,* 1894, Lansing, Michigan, Michigan Historical Collections, Bentley Historical Library, University of Michigan, pp. 25–27.

114Caroline Bartlett Crane, "The Individual Factor in Social Regeneration," *The New Unity,* 6 (August 1896): 382–84, Crane Papers.

115"If Women Vote," unidentified Louisville, Kentucky, newspaper, undated, Crane Papers; and Church Minutes, 17 May 1893, People's Church Library Archives, Kalamazoo, Michigan.

116"Treatment of Criminals," Kalamazoo *Daily Telegraph* (29 October 1892); "Denounced the Bill," unidentified Kalamazoo newspaper, undated, Crane Papers; and Church Minutes, 17 May 1893, People's Church Library Archives, Kalamazoo, Michigan.

117"Not Alms But a Friend," unidentified Kalamazoo newspaper, undated, Nell Hudson Scrapbooks, Crane Papers.

118"Mr. Bush's Trial," *Kalamazoo Gazette* (7 February 1896; University Microfilm: Ann Arbor, Michigan, available through Western Michigan University Library, Kalamazoo, Michigan); "Bush Still Boss," *Kalamazoo Gazette* (28 February 1896); "The Supervisor's Committee Report Against Superintendent Bush," *Kalamazoo Gazette* (17 January 1896).

119Tucker, *Prophetic Sisterhood*, p. 94.

120Church calendars for the months of November 1896 to March 1897; and Caroline Bartlett Crane and members of the Kalamazoo Unity Club, "A Study of the Social Conditions of Kalamazoo," unpublished, handwritten, and typescript reports, Crane Papers.

121Church calendar for November 1896, People's Church Archives, Crane Papers.

122Ahlstrom, *A Religious History of the American People*, pp. 796–97.

123Caroline Bartlett Crane, "Solid Chunks of Truth," reprint of a sermon on "Sullivanism," ca. 1896, Crane Papers.

124Crane, "The Story of an Institutional Church," p. 724.

125C. H. Cramer, *Royal Bob: The Life of Robert G. Ingersoll*, p. 161.

126Crane, "The Story and the Results," p. 18.

127"Have the Prayers Been Answered," *New York Journal* (13 January, 1896).

128"Its Deeds Suit Ingersoll," *Chicago Chronicle* (17 January 1896); "Ingersoll's Church," *New York Journal,* (16 January 1896); "Church that Suits Ingersoll," *New York World* (12 January 1896); "Col. Ingersoll is Winning," *Boston Herald* (13 January 1896).

129Caroline Bartlett Crane, "An Unsectarian Church," typescript "answer to scores of inquiries after the Ingersoll incident," Crane Papers; and "Story of Offer of Fellowship," *Chicago Tribune* (26 January 1896).

130"Story of Offer of Fellowship," *Chicago Tribune,* (26 January 1896).

131Robert G. Ingersoll to Caroline Bartlett, 24 January 1896, Crane Papers.

132"Bob is Not So Bad," *Kalamazoo Gazette* (20 January 1896); and "All People Agree," *Kalamazoo Daily Telegraph,* (20 January 1896).

133"Have the Prayers Been Answered," *New York Journal* (13 January 1896).

134Caroline Bartlett to Lorenzo and Louise Bartlett, 4 January 1892, Crane Papers.

135"As to Mr. Baker, His Seances Indicate No Supernatural Powers," unidentified Kalamazoo newspaper, undated, Nell Hudson Scrapbooks, Crane Papers.

136Interview, Roger Greeley, former minister of People's Church, Kalamazoo, Michigan; and Crane, "The Story of an Institutional Church," 731.

137William C. Huyser, "A. W. Crane, M. D.," a pamphlet of an address read at the Crane Memorial Meeting of the Kalamazoo Academy of Medicine, 21 December 1937, p. 2, Crane Papers; and the University of Michigan Department of Medicine and Surgery Commencement Program, 24 June 1894, Crane Papers; and People's Church calendar for March, 1895, reported that Augustus Warren Crane was the leader of the Young Men's Class.

138Warren Augustus Crane to Caroline Bartlett Crane, undated letter, ca. 1896, Crane Papers.

139"Becomes a Bride," *Kalamazoo Daily Telegraph* (2 January 1897).

TOWARD A NEW WAY OF LIFE

As a young girl Crane had spent time reading and studying rather than learning household skills, but after her marriage she recalled her vow to her mother, that if she did ever marry she would devote herself to learning domesticity.[1] Caroline and Warren, although far from wealthy, hired domestic help, but Caroline was not willing to sit idly by and watch her cook and housekeeper work. Each morning she held "cabinet" meetings with her domestic staff to plan the day's work,[2] including the meals, which were usually meatless. Caroline had become a vegetarian by the time of her marriage, and her husband suffered from gout and abstained from meat and other protein-rich foods.[3]

Her new role as a housekeeper inspired Caroline in 1897 to start the People's Church School of Household Science, which became the church's most successful institutional program.[4] The school which had an enrollment of ninety students, offered classes in cooking, housekeeping, home nursing, and sewing. Its teachers were vocational school graduates from Chicago, but because of a resignation, Crane was faced with teaching the housekeeping course during the school's first year. Feeling unprepared for such a duty, she devoted herself to study, and through studying and teaching the class, she became sensitive to environmental and food hygiene issues.[5] Crane also opened a Manual Training program for men, which taught carpentry and other trades, but it was less successful than the Household Science classes. Crane said she

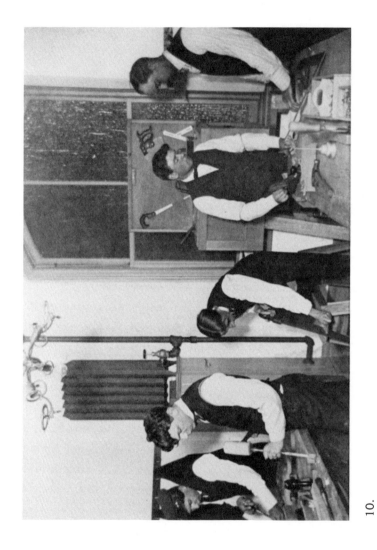

10.

A carpentry class at the School of Manual Science at People's Church.

11.

A junior sewing class at the School of Household Science at People's Church.

started the Manual Training school mainly to keep young men off the streets at night. After the Household Science and Manual Training programs had been operated for two years by People's Church, the Kalamazoo public school system adopted similar programs into its regular curriculum in 1899. Crane said her church had been "glad to have helped demonstrate to the public the practical educational value of vocational education."[6]

In 1899 the City of Kalamazoo also assumed control of the church's public kindergarten, which was one of the first in Michigan. In 1897 the church had opened a second kindergarten, located in an elementary school on Frank Street, as more than one hundred students were enrolled.[7] A year later the church announced it would donate all its kindergarten furniture to the city school system, and on June 5, 1899, voters approved making the kindergarten a part of the public school program.[8]

Meanwhile, on November 24, 1897, suffrage leaders Susan B. Anthony and Anna Howard Shaw spoke at People's Church and visited in the Crane home. At that time Anthony was president of the National American Woman's Suffrage Association and Shaw was vice president. A local newspaper reported that Crane and Anthony had enjoyed a close friendship for twelve years. Crane had met Shaw and Anthony for the first time when she was a young newspaper reporter during the 1885 suffrage convention in Minneapolis. At that time Anthony was the traveling advocate of suffrage, while Elizabeth Cady Stanton, who resigned as president of the suffrage organization in 1892, had been for many years the "inside" executive of the movement. Anthony maintained that if she had married she would not have been able to carry out her work.[9] A year earlier, approximately three weeks after Crane's marriage to Warren, Anthony expressed surprise at

Crane's decision to wed. Anthony wrote that she believed the marriage would interfere with Crane's career:

> Well, I cannot say whether I rejoice over the act until the time when we can tell whether the marriage proves to help you in your chosen profession. . . my feeling is that every woman who undertakes any sort of public life makes a mistake to adjust herself to too many dividing and distracting kinds of work through marriage . . . . I believe that marriage and maternity are professions by themselves, incompatible with what we would call a career! Either the house or the profession is more likely to suffer.[10]

Suffrage opponents claimed that suffragettes were less feminine and neglected their housemaking duties to work for the vote. But Anthony, in comments to the press in Kalamazoo, said that women still could be homemakers and work for women's suffrage. In praising women's domestic life, she said that "a mother must always hold her duty to children and home of first importance." Crane, in defending Anthony, said she was an "entirely womanly woman" and a "very competent house-keeper."[11]

All in all, the year 1897 was the most successful year in Crane's ministry. A study of the church calendar in 1897 shows an average of 118 meetings a month in the church.[12] This busy schedule and her new duties as a wife undoubtedly made Crane's life complex —and resulted in exhaustion. In her annual report sermon, on January 9, 1898, Crane told the congregation that she planned to resign in 1899, her tenth anniversary in the community.[13] In an article in the *Chicago Tribune* she said that she wanted to continue her education at the University of Chicago, taking graduate courses in sociology and practical settlement work.[14] She said she wanted the next year in the ministry—her last—to be the best year possible. But it turned out differently.

After an apparent power struggle with the church trustees, Crane presented her resignation to the church's board of trustees on April 5, 1898.[15] The minutes of the May 27 board meeting reveal a dispute over the authority to name the speaker for Sunday evening services.[16] Because church policy mandated that her resignation be presented first to the full congregation, the trustees refused to act on either her demand or her resignation.

A letter to the congregation dated May 26, 1898, however, said that her resignation was necessary because of poor health:

> My health has been so poor as to make it difficult for me to continue at work, and two months ago I felt obliged to notify the trustees of the church I must ask release in the near future, that is, at the end of the present church year, June 26.[17]

It continued with the explanation that she had not "at present sufficient self-control to make the announcement (from the pulpit) herself, and I shall attempt no farewell word later. What we have been to each other will be made neither greater nor less by pronouncing upon it." According to a newspaper report, Crane was not in her pulpit Sunday, May 29, when her resignation was announced.[18] Action by the congregation was scheduled at the June 6 meeting and accepted by the Board of Trustees' on June 7. The board also approved a resolution expressing its earnest wishes for "a full recovery of her former health and vigor."[19]

The *Kalamazoo Evening News* article attributed her resignation to "poor health" and reported that she had been "subject to an affliction of the heart which will prevent public speaking for some time to come." Crane hoped, the reporter noted, to recover her health by the fall so that she could begin "a course of advanced work in political economy and philosophy at Michigan University, and later in sociology and American constitutional history at the University of Chicago."

The precise nature of Crane's "poor health" is not entirely clear. She spoke in 1900 of "The Folly of Overwork" and said it had taken two years to recuperate;[20] in 1911, Belle C. LaFollette reported that Crane had had a "nervous breakdown" in 1898.[21] Whatever happened, it is obvious that this year marked a turning point in Crane's life. In addition to her marriage and her resignation from her ministry, Warren's father died shortly after their marriage, and his mother, Julia, became a member of their household until her death in 1919.[22]

To accommodate Julia or to have a place to which they could periodically retreat from her, Caroline and Warren purchased land at the north end of Gull Lake near Kalamazoo. At first, Caroline and Warren camped out at Gull Lake in a tent. Sometimes Caroline would walk alone along the shore, so Warren gave her a "pretty little Smith and Wesson" revolver. He insisted that she practice her aim by shooting at "little bobbing things in the water," and she wrote: "No man has yet been a candidate for killing, but I wear the pretty terror in my belt and the fame of my target practice goes abroad in my protection." The tent policeman was a half dollar placed on a table. If it was missing, the Cranes would immediately know someone had been at the camp. But none of their possessions were stolen.[23]

Around the turn of the century the Cranes constructed a small cottage on the site at Gull Lake, which they called "the Brown Thrush."[24] The cottage was so named because Warren thought it was like the "shy brown thrush in the green bushes skirting the lane to it," and Caroline agreed. The small cottage

12.

Dr. A. W. Crane is shown in a photograph taken probably when he was in Medical School at the University of Michigan.

had a large fireplace inside and wide porches outside. The spreading, curving roof was mossy green, and the sides were woodsy brown. The porches and trimmings were stained brown, also, and the doors and window sashes were a cheery yellow, Crane said.[25] In a romantic, handwritten account of their life at the cottage, Caroline revealed her love for the lake and her love and respect for her husband during those days of "mainly keeping company with her sweetheart." She wrote of her first impression of the lake: "Happily I felt instant captive of the charms of Gull Lake and was even the first to see gulls circling overhead against the sun, then soaring a while on the blue sky, with the sun caressing their splendid sweep."[26] Writing of her love of the open bedroom, she said:

> And we ascend those stairs to sleep with eyes naked to the zenith stars, without so much as a swaying bough between us and those august presence's by day, and shed such unearthly splendor over earthly night. Should it rain? The stars withdraw from the scene. And so can we. O, to live thus day and night in the fullness of earth and heaven!

Caroline said their life at the Brown Thrush was selfish: "We never entertain, but we sometimes love to have such friends about us as love not only us, but love the things we love—the Brown Thrush cottage with its fire and great glorious outdoors by day and night." Warren enjoyed fishing on the lake, and Caroline liked to hunt mushrooms and watch the stars from her sleeping verandah.[27] During their first summer at the cottage, Warren taught Caroline how to swim and how to ride "Billy," the pretty and rather spirited horse Warren drove when making his calls on patients. Billy was usually their means of transportation to the

13.

The Brown Thrush cottage at Gull Lake. This photograph was taken about 1905.

cottage.[28] The Cranes frequently spent Sundays, and usually a month during the summer, at the cottage.

During the spring of 1899, Caroline traveled by train to La Jolla, California, where she spent more than two months recuperating from her "nervous breakdown."[29] Crane's letters during this period are not available. Warren's are, however, and they reveal a very loving and passionate relationship. In a letter written by Warren while Caroline was in California, he said he "longed to put my face between your lovely breasts."[30] On another occasion he wrote, "O, Dearie, the different places I shall place my thirsty lips in quivering delight."[31] Caroline planned to return to Kalamazoo via Chicago, after stopping to visit her father and stepmother in Keokuk. Warren anxiously awaited her return, and they agreed to meet in Chicago and then return to Kalamazoo together. About their meeting in Chicago, he wrote: "To have a tryst with you, sweet lady, in another city, intoxicates my senses with rare witchery of romantic love."[32]

Warren's letters also brought Caroline medical advice: "You must not go into a mountainous district. It will add a strain to your heart and retard your recovery." He was concerned about her nervous condition and her left eye. "The nervous system once exhausted requires a long period of rest," he added. Caroline wore a pad over her left eye while she was in California. This was the first mention in their correspondence of the eye problem that would plague Caroline throughout her life. In addition, Warren's letters advised Caroline of the news at home. By 1899, People's Church had fallen on hard times. Warren wrote Caroline that the new pastor was a failure and only forty people attended Sunday services. The church was divided over the value of Christian Science theology, and in the spring of 1899 the new pastor resigned. Although Christian Scientists had been welcome to attend her services, Crane thought that the philosophy was "neither scientific nor Christian."[33]

Warren also expressed his desire to have children:

> How increasingly wonderful would be a child that were a reproduction of you and me combined. To think! Your Child! I it's father! But darling you are infinitely more precious than any child. Whatsoever, I truly want a child chiefly because you want it so.[34]

By this time Caroline was forty years old, and her age may have been a factor in their childlessness. Soon after his marriage, Warren became one of America's pioneer radiologists, many of whom became sterile because of the lack of protection from x-ray radiation. However, a physician who practiced with Warren during the 1930s said Crane claimed to have undergone extensive tests to prove he was not sterile.[35]

Back in 1896, Warren had read an Associated Press wire report that announced the discovery of a new invisible ray that allowed one to look "through a box and see an iron weight." Later that year he ordered his first x-ray equipment—a direct current induction coil, two primitive Crookes tubes, and a hand fluoroscope. He made his first x-rays in March 1897, and within the next two years he established himself as one of the most innovative roentgenologists, as early radiologists called themselves.[36]

Later medical historians credited Warren with several innovations in the x-ray's electrical apparatus, tube, and screen. Early in his use of the x-ray for diagnosis, Warren was particularly interested in using diagnostic chest x-rays. But his original screen was only 5" wide and 7" in length, allowing only for plates of broken bones and joint dislocations. To make chest x-rays possible, he had a manufacturer construct a screen that was 16" by 18". Desiring to conserve the new screen, he covered it with glass and sealed paraffin. Later he discovered that both the size of the screen and its glass cover protected him from harmful dosages of the invisible ray.[37] For Warren, the x-ray was mainly an important tool in diagnosis, and he later became a pioneer in the diagnosis of ulcers and stomach and intestinal cancer.[38] In 1899, Warren's pioneer work in chest roentgenology earned him membership in the London Roentgen Society; he was only the second American to receive such an honor, which was accorded him for a comprehensive journal article that a noted radiological historian said in 1934 "still stood as a model for guidance in fluoroscopy of the chest."[39]

The medical laboratory was another important tool in Warren's early practice. Bacteriology was a new science when Warren attended the University of Michigan, and he operated the first medical laboratory in Kalamazoo.[40] During his early years of practice in the city Warren put his knowledge to use as the city's bacteriologist, responsible for treatment and quarantine of people infected with communicable diseases. While Caroline was in California the city was struck by a typhoid fever epidemic. Warren, the city's chief medical officer, contracted the disease, and a policeman stood by his door to prevent him from leaving his home. Authorities feared that Warren, in his devotion to duty, would continue his rounds even while he was infected with the fever.[41]

Caroline continued to regain her strength, and by the fall of 1900 she was ready to return to an active life. In a speech at the Milwaukee Biennial of the General Federation of Women's Clubs in October, she warned other clubwomen of the folly of overwork that had "enforced her idleness."[42] Although she had resigned her pastorate at People's Church, she had not resigned from the ministry altogether. In 1901 she preached regularly at the Grand Rapids Unitarian Church while it searched for a regular minister,[43] and in 1903 she committed herself to a brief pastorate of the Unitarian congregation in Jackson, Michigan.[44] During these years she continued to write and publish religious articles and preach elsewhere when asked.

NOTES

[1]Caroline Bartlett Crane, "Housekeeping After Marriage," 1934 typescript recollections, p. 1, Crane Papers.

[2]Helen Christine Bennett, "Caroline Bartlett Crane of Kalamazoo: The First Municipal Expert of America," *Pictorial Review* (September 1910): 63.

[3]Crane, "Housekeeping After Marriage," p. 3.

[4]Crane, "Housekeeping After Marriage," p. 1.

[5]Crane, "Housekeeping After Marriage," p. 2.

[6]Crane, "Story of an Institutional Church," p. 2.

[7]"Annual 1897 Report," People's Church, Kalamazoo, Michigan, Crane Papers.

[8]"Minutes of the Kalamazoo Board of Education from 1882–1901," p. 641, Kalamazoo Board of Education Administration Building.

[9]"Susan B. Anthony: This Remarkable Woman Was in the City Last Wednesday Evening," *Kalamazoo Times,* (28 November 1897).

[10]Susan B. Anthony to Caroline Bartlett Crane, 21 January 1897, Crane Papers.

11"Susan B. Anthony: This Remarkable Woman Was in the City Last Wednesday Evening," *Kalamazoo Times,* (28 November 1897).

12Church calendars for 1897, People's Church, Kalamazoo, Michigan, Crane Papers.

13"Annual 1897 Report," People's Church, The Annual Sermon by Caroline Bartlett Crane, delivered 8 January 1898, p. 50.

14"Will Widen Her Field," *Chicago Tribune* (17 January 1898).

15Church Minutes, Board of Trustees, 5 April 1898, People's Church Library Archives.

16Church Minutes, Board of Trustees, 27 May 1898, People's Church Library Archives.

17Caroline Bartlett Crane to Board of Trustees, People's Church, 26 May 1898, handwritten letter of resignation, Crane Papers.

18"Quits Her Work," *Kalamazoo Evening News* (8 June 1898).

19Church Minutes, Board of Trustees, 7 June 1898, People's Church Library Archives.

20Caroline Bartlett Crane, "The Folly of Overwork," *Club Woman* 7 (October 1900): 5–7. The article is a transcript of her speech before the Milwaukee Biennial meeting of the General Federation of Women's Clubs in the autumn of 1900.

21Belle C. LaFollette, "Woman of the Hour: Caroline Bartlett Crane," *LaFollette* 3 (29 May 1911): 11.

22"Mother of Dr. A. W. Crane Has Resided Here Since 1897," *Kalamazoo Gazette* (1 April 1920); and "Killed by a Cave In," unidentified Adrian, Michigan newspaper, undated. Article tells of the death of Nathan Crane on June 19, 1897, in his Colorado mine, Crane Papers.

23Caroline Bartlett Crane, "The Brown Thrush," handwritten manuscript, 1906, Crane Papers, p. 48..

24Crane, "The Brown Thrush," p. 3.

25Crane, "The Brown Thrush," p. 53.

26Crane, "The Brown Thrush," pp. 110–12; Caroline Bartlett Crane to Augustus Warren Crane, 19 October 1908; Caroline Bartlett Crane to Augustus Warren Crane, 23 November 1908; and Caroline Bartlett Crane to Augustus Warren Crane, 27 September 1906, Crane Papers.

27Crane, "The Brown Thrush," p. 48.

28Caroline Bartlett Crane, "The Brown Thrush," 1934 typescript recollection, Crane Papers, p. 2.

29Numerous letters from Augustus Warren Crane to Caroline Bartlett Crane written between March and June 1899, Crane Papers.

30Augustus Warren Crane to Caroline Bartlett Crane, 12 April 1899, Crane Papers.

31Augustus Warren Crane to Caroline Bartlett Crane, 15 April 1899, Crane Papers.

32Augustus Warren Crane to Caroline Bartlett Crane, 17 April 1899, Crane Papers.

33Caroline Bartlett Crane, "Christian Science," *Unity* 47 (1901): 53.

34Augustus Warren Crane to Caroline Bartlett Crane, 29 April 1899, Crane Papers.

35Interview, Dr. Roscoe Hildreth, Kalamazoo, Michigan, 6 April 1985.

36Augustus Warren Crane to Dr. Preston M. Hickey, 3 November 1927, as cited by Howard P. Doub in "Augustus Crane: 1868–1937," *Radiology* 65 (July 1955): 3.

[37]William A. Evans, "Michigan's Contribution to Early Roentgenology," *Journal of the Michigan State Medical Society* (May 1934): 13.

[38]Evans, "Michigan's Contribution to Early Roentgenology," 12.

[39]Evans, "Michigan's Contribution to Early Roentgenology," 15.

[40]William C. Huyser, "A. W. Crane, M. D.", (Kalamazoo: Kalamazoo Academy of Medicine), p. 2, Crane Papers.

[41]Warren Augustus Crane to Caroline Bartlett Crane, 11 April 1912, Crane Papers; and Rush McNair, *Medical Memoirs of 50 Years in Kalamazoo* (Kalamazoo: by the author, 1938), p. 83.

[42]Crane, "The Folly of Overwork," p. 5.

[43]"The Source of Faith," *Grand Rapids Democrat* (14 January 1901); and Crane, "Biographical Sketch," 1933 unpublished typescript, p. 7, Crane Papers.

[44]"Brilliant Woman," *Jackson Michigan Evening Press* (12 June 1903).

MUNICIPAL REFORMS

By 1901, Crane had fully recovered her health. She devoted the next two years to two municipal housekeeping crusades, first in Kalamazoo and eventually throughout the state: meat hygiene reform and improved health care for poorhouse patients. Crane became sensitive to the need for improved meat hygiene while teaching a course in housekeeping at the People's Church School of Household Science.[1] She taught her students that they had a duty to be careful in selecting food for their families. In like manner, she believed that a municipal housekeeper should be vigilant against the entry of unhygienic food, especially meat, into the community marketplaces. She was named chairman of the State GFWC's Household Economics Committee in 1901, and she wrote a course on municipal housekeeping, which was published in pamphlet form. Among many diverse crusades and civic improvement projects, Crane considered her struggle for meat hygiene her most important contribution to society.

The first episode in Crane's battle for a healthful meat supply occurred as she prepared to teach a course in municipal housekeeping at her own women's organization, The Kalamazoo Twentieth Century Club. One of the class's sessions was entitled "A Petition from the Kitchen to the City Council For the Inspection of Milk and Mcat." Crane was reluctant to pose as an expert on the topics so she persuaded a local physician to discuss the milk problem. She could find no one, however, who could talk with authority on meat hygiene.[2]

Crane believed the topic deserved more in-depth coverage than a layman such as she could provide, and to secure the needed information she decided to survey the local slaughterhouses. Crane invited two men and two women, one of them the wife of the current mayor and the other the wife of a former mayor, to accompany her. Crane and her entourage spent the better part of two days—March 21 and 22, 1902—inspecting the seven small slaughterhouses located within a mile of Kalamazoo.[3]

She found deplorable conditions. None of the slaughter-houses had provisions for drainage, and Crane recorded that the "earth beneath and around is soaked with the rotted blood and filth of many years." She added:

> The pens and sheds containing the animals to be slaughtered are for the most part, apparently bottomless pits of mud and filth into which the half-devoured, uncooked offal is trampled, while squealing pigs carry on, literally, an intestine warfare; presenting, when it is remembered that these same swine are destined shortly to be eaten by ourselves, a sight as revolting as human imagination could picture. In one pen we saw trampled into the mud the decomposing body of a very small calf, quite too young, I think, to have been born, and inevitably suggesting the previous slaughter of a pregnant animal.[4]

Furthermore, the buildings were old wooden barns or sheds, unpainted, weather-beaten, and decaying. With only one exception, all were "filthy to an unspeakable and unimaginable degree." Rats inhabited every slaughterhouse, and only a "hoe and plane with long conscientious application" could have removed from the walls, floor, posts, and shelves the "caked blood, grime, grease, hair, mold, and other quite unmentionable filth which covers every inch of exposed surface. . . ." The tools used to slaughter and dress the animals were no better than the surroundings. Invariably Crane found filthy knives, saws, and cleavers. "It is perhaps needless to add that the hands and clothing of the butchers were as filthy as their filthy methods and surroundings," she wrote.[5]

Following the second day of investigation Crane took a train to Chicago, where she visited a large packinghouse that was under government inspection. There she viewed slaughtering methods similar to those she had observed in Kalamazoo, but in Chicago she found them performed quite "decently, cleanly, and with proper sanitary safeguards."[6] She restricted her inquiries and observations to the inspection of animals at the time of slaughter and to the sanitation of the facilities where the slaughtering and dressing of the fresh carcasses took place. These were the operations she had observed at home; as yet she had no reason to investigate whether the animals were fit for slaughter in the first place, which became the focus of a later crusade.

When she returned to Kalamazoo, Crane contacted all the local butchers who purchased meat from the unclean slaughterhouses and found them openly hostile to the suggestion of reform. On March 25, a newspaper reporter overheard the private protestations of one of the butchers about Crane's investigations, and that evening the lead story of the *Kalamazoo Evening Telegraph* was headlined, "Foul Places."[7] Crane had hoped to keep her investigations quiet, at least until she had met with the butchers. The article featured interviews with the mayor and the city health officer and carried the prediction that there would be a "move to inspect meats" and to establish a central abattoir, the word for slaughterhouse commonly used at the turn of the century.

Butchers and meat dealers were infuriated. Crane already had a reputation as a "meddler," and obviously the article destroyed her hopes for an amicable conference with them. Only four meat dealers—and no butchers—attended the conference, and only one of the meat dealers showed any interest in reform.[8] The next day, March 26, the Twentieth Century Club held its regular meeting, and Crane spoke to a full house, including the mayor, the health officer, and a number of physicians. Crane told of her shock at the filth that prevailed in the slaughterhouses; of the primitive nature of the seven structures she visited; of the revolting meat-handling habits in all of them; of the lack of even the most basic regulations for handling the meat; and of the indifference to this situation displayed by those directly involved. Reaction from the clubwomen was strong, and they approved a resolution supporting reform in unequivocal terms.[9]

Failing in her attempt to meet with the tradesmen, Crane drafted a letter to each of them that asked them to construct a common, sanitary slaughterhouse, or, if that were not possible, to acquire a water supply and clean up their individual operations. She also suggested that they ask the city to license slaughterhouses, hire a meat inspector, and approve regulations that would allow consumers to have confidence in the safety of their meat supply. Such a move, Crane said, would bring local slaughterhouses and meat markets to the level of those in Chicago. She concluded her letter:

> If there is anything belonging to women's sphere surely it is the wholesomeness and cleanliness of the food she sets before her family. This is what I think the women of Kalamazoo are determined to see to. If we have to get our meat

from a distance we will do it. But if the butchers will effect
what we ask, the Chicago packinghouses will find a fast
diminishing field in this part of Michigan, and our own trade
will correspondingly increase with a just reputation for
enterprise and reasonable regard for the health and welfare of
our own people.[10]

Receiving no response, Crane attended the Kalamazoo
City Council meeting the following week. Accompanied by a
committee of women from the Twentieth Century Club, she
argued at length for municipal meat standards. Her request for
local meat inspection was heard with some favor and was referred
to a committee composed of the city attorney, health officer, and
herself. The group was directed to write an ordinance for meat
inspection.[11]

But the committee was fighting stiff odds. At the turn of
the century Michigan and most other states limited the powers of
cities and towns. Later, home rule for cities became an important
issue nationwide as cities grew and urban problems mounted. The
city attorney advised the Kalamazoo City Council that it lacked
the power to pass a meat inspection law because the city charter
gave Kalamazoo no control over slaughterhouses. The only
answer was an act of the state legislature,[12] but it would be a year
before that body met again. Meanwhile, Crane urged local citizens
to boycott local meat and to purchase only meat that bore the
federal inspection stamp. So many citizens took her advice that
some meat dealers began to advertise that they handled only
federally inspected meat.[13]

Crane found the Michigan State Board of Health
especially helpful as she gathered information on writing a state
law that would give cities more home-rule powers over meat
inspection. She had become convinced that unsanitary meat was a

statewide problem from evidence she gathered as she traveled to other cities, including Detroit and Lansing, where conditions were similar to those in Kalamazoo. She sent letters of inquiry to secretaries of state and boards of health throughout the nation, and thus found that most states had no effective meat supply regulation and that only a few cities had mostly ineffective meat inspection laws.[14]

Crane's work for a Michigan law gained the support of the State Board of Health, and in February 1903 she was asked to speak before an annual state conference of health officials. The group supported her enthusiastically and appointed a committee to write a bill to be offered to the legislature, which by then was in session. The chairman of the committee, however, was too busy to call a meeting. With the deadline fast approaching, Crane wrote the proposal on her own, with the help of a Kalamazoo attorney.[15]

Her bill faced immediate difficulty because of another proposal drafted by a veterinarian lobby, a bill that seems to have been introduced to provide more meat inspection work for veterinarians. Crane traveled to Lansing four times before her bill was reported out of committee and passed by the Senate. She returned home, having arranged with legislative supporters that she would return when her bill came up in the House. However, a change in the House calendar brought the bill to final passage more quickly than expected. Because the bill did not specifically exclude the right of farmers to slaughter their animals in barns, the farm lobby managed to defeat it.[16]

Crane received news of the bill's defeat at six o'clock the next morning and was on the next train to Lansing. She worked throughout the day to find a legislator who had voted against the bill to move for its reconsideration, which was possible only within twenty-four hours of the bill's defeat. She also managed to meet with the Speaker of the House, who became interested in her cause and allowed Crane five minutes to speak on the House floor. An amendment was added to appease the farm lobby and, by a single vote, the House approved a motion for reconsideration. The bill was placed on the calendar for the opening of the next day's session. Crane worked furiously until midnight to win supporters. She toiled through the night and into the morning to prepare statements that were placed on each legislator's desk. When the bill was called, its friends were so numerous and so kind that, Crane said, she "feared that it would be talked to death." But it was not. By a 66–19 vote, the bill received House approval and was promptly signed into law by the governor.[17]

Crane's law allowed cities, villages, and townships to inspect all animals intended for meat supplies in their jurisdictions and to inspect all meat slaughtered elsewhere but sold by local butchers. Units of local government could also regulate slaughter-houses and meat markets, and, if they desired, license the sale of meat, build a public slaughterhouse, and regulate its usage. In addition to the general state law Crane also championed a special law, stronger than the general one, for the City of Kalamazoo.[18] She believed this effort would give Kalamazoo the most perfect system of meat inspection of any city in the state, if not the nation. Almost immediately after the general law passed, the State Board of Health asked Crane to write a model ordinance that could be passed by local governments. With the assistance of a deputy attorney general she drafted the model, which was endorsed by the State Board of Health and was ready for use the day the new law went into effect, September 17, 1903. On that same day Crane received a telegram from the Saginaw, Michigan, City Council asking her to address their group and to investigate local meat conditions.[19] The City Federation of Women's Clubs and the local medical society were well represented at the meeting. Later, forty-two physicians petitioned the council in favor of meat inspection regulations. Crane's model ordinance was introduced, and it appeared that Saginaw would be the first Michigan city to enact an ordinance under provisions of one of Crane's laws. Unfortunately, the mayor gave ear to the objections of local butchers and invited them to write an ordinance instead. A long, hard battle was waged by both sides, and Crane had trouble identifying the remains of her model ordinance in the law Saginaw finally put in place.[20]

She consoled herself with the knowledge that only eighteen months earlier there had been no state laws; now there were two. Her thoughts turned homeward, where public sentiment and the newspapers clearly were on her side. Crane was granted another Kalamazoo City Council hearing, which she attended armed with a petition that "reached across the council chamber and back." But the petitioners were women. At the next meeting, her opponents brought a petition with only a quarter as many names but all male signatures. At the public hearing on the following Monday, Crane saw the council chambers crowded with men, mainly butchers and meat dealers, with two attorneys they had employed to assist them in their fight. Crane was the lone woman present, and she was supported only by her husband. Crane argued that the slaughterhouses were filthy places and that all citizens were endangered by diseased meat. Her foes raged that imposing a license upon butchers was unconstitutional. The butchers were irate over the meddlesomeness of a woman and were critical of the medical profession, mainly because Dr. Crane was present. The battle lasted until nearly one o'clock in the morning. After more than five hours, the council decided it was best not to make a decision in the heat of battle.[21]

Eventually Crane lost the fight in Kalamazoo, but she was gaining notoriety elsewhere. The task of answering her correspondence became overwhelming as she sought information on meat inspection from American and European sources. In the fall of 1903 she persuaded the Michigan State Board of Health to conduct an evening workshop on meat inspection for state and county health officials. Crane recruited the speakers, and on January 7, 1904, the program was held in Ann Arbor in the amphitheater of the University of Michigan's new medical building. Four speakers, including university medical professors and herself, gave lectures.[22]

Even during the time when her campaign for meat hygiene achieved state recognition, Crane's attentions were being drawn to another cause. In April, 1903, she began a long campaign to improve medical care in the poorhouses. She received a complaint from a local citizen about conditions at the Kalamazoo County Poorhouse, and, as she was to do many times in the future, she decided to investigate for herself.

The conditions she found and the lack of nursing care, in particular, distressed her: women rotting from bed sores, an infant with syphilis, a man who had been in bed for twelve years. This man left his bed only on the rare occasions when a harness was used to hoist him up; his arms and legs were distorted out of human resemblance and his jaws were twisted so tightly that he could hardly open them to eat. He was appreciative of Crane's attention when she washed him.[23]

When Crane revealed her findings to the Board of County Supervisors, the panel granted her request to hire a temporary nurse for the poorhouse. But that improvement was short-lived. At a public meeting the keeper and the matron of the facility complained about the "extry wash" that resulted from the nurse's insistence on bathing the sick. The board terminated the temporary nurse because of the discord she caused and in order to save the high cost of her wages, $10 monthly.[24]

In 1902 the medical appropriation for the Kalamazoo poorhouse was $100 of the total $16,000 budget. That year a total of eighty-six persons were admitted to the poorhouse and eleven died. According to a state report, the most common causes for admission to poorhouses were unemployment (mostly among the elderly), sickness, insanity, homelessness, physical impairments, and retardation.[25]

Crane spoke on poorhouse reform at the 1903 Annual Convention of the Michigan State Conference of Charities and Corrections and County Agents, a gathering to which she was a delegate for several years. Crane urged fellow delegates involved in state and private charity work to inspect poorhouses in their own communities. She concluded:

> If we have a sick dog, we either tend it, cleanse its sores, and see to its needs, or, we put it out of its misery. Our consciences rightly revolt at the latter alternative for any human being, however sick and miserable. But how can we then escape the other alternative of rationally and humanely caring for these charges upon human society! If there are any curses that God hears, it must be the curses of these poor stranded wrecks, abandoned to die without let or hindrance, and cursing society, which has paid them back in their same unsocial and anti-social coin, and bettered the bargain!![26]

At Crane's suggestion, the Michigan State Federated Women's Clubs created the Almshouse Committee in 1904, and she was named chairwoman.[27] After making a comprehensive survey of the state's poorhouses, she proposed that the eleven thousand club women in Michigan create a system for performing, and then themselves perform, inspections of pauper, penal, and charitable institutions. Crane devised a questionnaire, and women in each county conducted investigations and returned the questionnaire to Crane. She told the State Conference of Charities and Corrections that the inspections were "preeminently a work for women, because they as mothers, as housekeepers, as natural and practical nurses, and as the sex having the most leisure, are best fitted for the work."[28]

Crane's unsuccessful reform campaigns in Kalamazoo led her to organize a group to provide support in her municipal improvement endeavors. In the fall of 1903 Crane organized the Kalamazoo Women's Civic Improvement League, and for the next three years this group was the center of her work. The formation of a league was not a new idea as, as early as the 1870s, women throughout the nation were organizing into improvement societies and civic leagues and becoming active in municipal housekeeping projects.[29] Kalamazoo's league, however, was unusually sophisticated for a small city.

To form the group, Crane sent letters to the Ladies' Literary Association and to the Twentieth Century Club suggesting the appointment of a joint committee to consider organizing a Women's Civic Improvement League.[30] She worked furiously during the next two months to found the WCIL in January 1904. In addition to the Ladies' Literary Association and the Twentieth Century Club, several other groups joined the league, including the Women's Christian Temperance Union, the Celery City Club (an organization of black women), the Daughters of the American Revolution, and the women's societies from the Episcopal, Methodist, Baptist, Jewish, Congregational, and People's churches.[31] Jewish and Black support aside, the WCIL was predominately a white, Protestant, middle class organization. Catholic women were noticeably absent from its membership rolls, mainly because of the oppostion of the Kalamazoo priest, Reverend Frank A. O'Brien, to Crane's work. Reverend O'Brien apparently thought that Catholic women should devote their time to Catholic charities and church work.[32] At first the WCIL membership was comprised of women's clubs and individual women. Men could purchase associate memberships, and children were organized into a Junior Civic Improvement League.

The WCIL's first public health project was to hire a visiting nurse to attend to the needs of the city's poor and elderly. During the first two years of the program the nurse made more than five thousand home visits. Her case load ranged from new mothers and their babies to elderly people who were bed-ridden and suffering. Much of her work, however, was in public health education. She gave instructions in household sanitation, personal hygiene, and cooking and diet. In addition, she provided the sick with clean clothing, bed linen, and food.[33] Major support for the nurse's work came from donations and league membership fees. Patients were asked to pay for service according to their ability, and frequently the fees collected were so small as to pay not even the "incidental expenses" of a visit. Fees ranged from a nickel to a quarter, with patients rarely paying more than ten cents; in the home of a destitute no fee was charged.[34]

The nurse was particularly useful in helping indigent mothers and their infants recover from childbirth complications. Crane reported that the nurse saved the eyesight of several infants born with eye infections, frequently gave baths to reduce the temperature of patients with typhoid fever, and was vigilant in reporting tuberculosis and other contagious diseases to physicians. In addition, the visiting nurse reported unemployment, violations of community sanitation regulations, school truancy, juvenile delinquency, and child labor law violations to WCIL headquarters.[35]

The Kalamazoo WCIL was best known for its municipal housekeeping activism, and at the group's inception Crane served as chairwoman of its public health committee. At one of the first meetings in 1904 she showed lantern slides she had taken of the city's alleys and backyards.[36] Her audience squirmed at the abhorrent conditions Crane presented. A cleanup campaign was initiated, and the WCIL, cooperating with the city's Commercial Club, organized cleanup days for several years.[37] This initial success paved the way for a more grandiose project in the spring of 1904. Representing the WCIL, Crane petitioned the city commission for permission to take charge of the cleaning of six blocks of Main Street (now Michigan Avenue) in the heart of the downtown business district, for three months, beginning May 2.[38]

Before beginning the project, the WCIL investigated street cleaning techniques employed by other cities and came to the conclusion that a system created by noted sanitary engineer George E. Waring in 1895 was probably the most efficient and cost effective. Because of Waring's reforms in New York City, the city employed more than five thousand street sweepers and garbage collectors.[39] The salient features of the system included white uniformed street sweepers called "White Wings," who used push brooms to collect street dirt into piles. They then swept the piles into bags suspended upon two-wheeled bag carriers.[40] The three White Wings that the WCIL hired for Kalamazoo patrolled assigned areas. The Waring System also called for the pavement to be flushed down by the Fire Department at least once a week. In Kalamazoo, however, the firemen had neither the knowledge nor the enthusiasm for performing this task. The first few times the

streets were flushed Crane arose at three o'clock in the morning to
supervise the firemen and make sure that the streets were flushed
from the center out to the gutters. The excess water was scrubbed
from between the bricks in the pavement. Later, when the mud
had dried, the White Wings were to sweep it up and bag it. The
sweepings were later sold for fertilizer.

Streetsweeping was only one element of Crane's plan; the
WCIL was successful in pressuring the city commission to enact an
anti-spitting ordinance. Because the city made little effort to
enforce it, however, the women took it upon themselves to patrol
the streets, reporting to the city attorney all offenders, particularly
those who deposited tobacco onto the pavement. To remedy a
littering problem, Crane had trash cans placed at frequent intervals
along Main Street.[41] Youngsters from the Junior Civic Improvement League distributed flyers asking people not to litter and sang
songs about sanitation—with lyrics written by Crane—to generate
civic awareness. One of the songs was sung to the tune of
"Yankee Doodle":

> There was a man in our town
> And he was wondrous wise;
> He threw some paper in the street,
> Right front of people's eyes!
> And when he saw that paper there,
> With all his might and main,
> He jumped into the street—he did—
> And picked it up again!
>
> He put that paper in the can,
> As every man should do, Sir;
> He went and joined the Civic League
> And was that wise man you, Sir?[42]

Crane's songs were on the lips of many citizens, from the youngest child to the oldest citizen; and by July 1 more than thirty cans stood along the league's six blocks of Main Street. But at that time the street cleaning portion of the project failed. Everything went well for the first eight weeks, but then the sweepers' brooms wore out. Crane believed the street commissioner had sabotaged the project by deliberately failing to order enough brooms.[43] A bloc of city aldermen wanted to return to the old method of sweeping the streets with a machine that used hard wire brushes. On June 20, the WCIL terminated its contract with the city because of the dispute over the brooms, and within a few days the city ordered a new streetsweeping machine and sprinkler at the enormous cost of $1,015.

Crane did not take the defeat easily. She contended that the city's new system was economically inefficient, that the sprinkler caused the pavements to deteriorate, that the sweeper's wire brushes wore out the streets, and that dust raised by the brushes increased citizens' chances for tuberculosis, pneumonia, and influenza.[44]

Determined that street cleaning would be done her way, Crane and her sanitary vigilantes applied pressure on the politically sensitive commissioners. By that time, the WCIL was a political force to contend with, representing three hundred women and men active in civic affairs. In August the aldermen finally admitted they had been wrong and vowed to reinstitute the Waring system.[45]

For two months, beginning in late August, 1904, Crane escaped the streetsweeping struggle to visit relatives in Iowa. When she returned to Kalamazoo she discovered that the city's heart still was not in the WCIL street-cleaning plan. The old machine sweeper was forever coming along to help the men who had neglected their work, and men were shifted here and there as it happened. The streets were not flushed regularly. Eventually, she grew to accept the limited success of the Waring system in Kalamazoo.[46]

Other Kalamazoo WCIL public health projects that year included a survey of housing conditions and an effort to reform the unsanitary method by which bread was distributed in the community. The housing survey located over-crowded areas and houses with poor lighting and sanitation. Thanks to the clean bread project bread distributors began wrapping each loaf before it was delivered to store shelves.[47] At that time, Crane's Junior Civic League had as many as a thousand members. The children were given prizes in contests for lawn care, gardening, and flower bed design.[48] Crane also helped form a Civic Improvement League in Comstock, a small rural town in Kalamazoo County. Her work in that community was responsible for several civic improvements and the organization of the first consolidated rural school district in Michigan.[49]

In 1905 the Women's Civic Improvement League organized a Charity Organization Committee to systematize public and private charity relief by means of a central office and bureau of registration. The centralization would, they hoped, secure some degree of harmony and cooperation among the various charitable organizations in the community—cooperation that would reduce fraud and duplication of relief efforts.[50]

Crane served as chairwoman of the Charity Organization for its first three years. She convinced the city that operating the organization was in Kalamazoo's best interest. The city, in turn, said it would pay the salary of a secretary to oversee the organization's office.[51] The WCIL visiting nurse lived in the headquarters building and provided additional staff expertise.

One of the Charity Organization's important projects was establishing an Employment Bureau, to work toward finding employment for the community's able-bodied men and women. If the bureau could not find work for men who desired relief, the men were sent to the Charity Organization's Woodyard. In payment for their labors there, the Charity Organization wrote tickets for groceries, shoes, and clothing, which could be redeemed in local stores. Women in similar circumstances were paid for working in a sewing center.[52]

The Woodyard probably discouraged railroad hoboes from stopping in Kalamazoo. According to railroad company records about half a million hoboes rode the nation's rails at the turn of the century. Crane urged housewives to refuse to feed hoboes who strayed from the tracks in Kalamazoo and to advise them of the existence of the Woodyard. Furthermore, she sought and secured some improvement on the part of the railroad companies in policing their tracks against the tramp problem.[53]

During this time Crane had become closely associated with the leaders of social work journalism, Paul and Arthur Kellogg, who had been newspaper reporters and editors in Kalamazoo. Paul Kellogg left Kalamazoo in 1902 to attend Columbia University. When he first arrived in New York, he found a part-time job working for the New York Charity Organization's *Charities* magazine. Eventually Arthur joined his brother at the magazine, which would later become *The Survey*.[54] Crane also associated with many social work experts. The noted New York tenement house reformer, Jacob Riis, came to Kalamazoo in 1905. He complimented the WCIL organization and praised Crane for her charity work and her efforts to reform poorhouse health care.[55]

In addition, she was becoming widely known as a lecturer. Crane first spoke at Carnegie Music Hall in New York City on February 26, on "The Higher Education of Women Considered as a Preparation for Life."[56] In March 1905 she gave three lectures in New York City sponsored by the Ethical Culture Society and the New York School of Philanthropy. Felix Adler, who was educated as an orthodox Hebrew rabbi, founded the Ethical Culture Society and was widely known for his social reforms. He was credited with starting the first free public kindergarten and creating the first visiting nurses' association in the United States. The Ethical Culture Society was composed of former members of the Jewish religion.

Later in the fall of 1905 Crane spoke at the American Civic Association's annual convention in Cleveland. Her talk was entitled "Juvenile Civic League Work," and it contended that children should be trained to have a "civic consciousness."[57] Soon after its organization the Kalamazoo WCIL joined the American Civic Association, which was concerned with improving urban life.[58] Under the leadership of Horace McFarland, the American Civic Association had been formed via the merger of the American Park and Outdoor Art Association and the American League of Civic Improvement. According to the new organization's earliest publication, its purpose was the "promotion of city, town, and neighborhood improvement" as well as the provision of leadership in the City Beautiful movement.

Between lectures Crane continued her crusade for meat hygiene reform. During the winter of 1904 she received an invitation to speak about meat inspection to a woman's club in Big Rapids, Michigan, a city of six thousand. Crane agreed to speak under one stipulation: the women must follow her example and make unannounced visits to slaughterhouses there. They must be accompanied by city officials, and if they found unsanitary conditions, they must pledge to work until the slaughterhouses were clean. The day before Crane's arrival three women, escorted by the mayor, made their rounds and found horrendous conditions. One butcher was cutting up a carcass so evidently diseased that, in his confusion, he could only think to say that he did not plan to sell it; he merely planned to feed it to his family. As a result of the club's patrol, the meeting mushroomed into a community meeting with a number of city officials present. A woman who had never summoned the courage to let her voice be heard in the ordinary club meetings rose and gave a vivid and moving report on behalf of her committee. On the spot, the women's club members decided they would buy no more meat from filthy slaughterhouses.[59]

A few days later, one of the butchers placed a notice in the newspaper that he planned to provide better meat for his customers as soon as he could raise the money to improve conditions at his slaughterhouse. Fortunately for the city and for the butcher, the mayor had recently inherited a considerable amount of money and pledged to finance the butcher's ambition. The mayor's inheritance constructed a model plant of cement and steel in the heart of the little city, despite opposition from the city council that the odor would discourage people from shopping downtown.

As a result of her efforts Crane was becoming widely known in the butcher trade. One day in the spring of 1904 she saw a notice in the local newspaper that the secretary of The Master Butchers of America, a trade organization, was to be in Kalamazoo to organize a local branch of that society. She invited the secretary and his wife to her home and talked with them at length, trying to convince them that she was really working in the butchers' best interest. Impressed with Crane's idea that local butchers could benefit from upgrading their meat supply in order to compete with the large meat-packing trust, the secretary invited her to speak before the organization's annual congress, to be held in St. Louis during the World's Fair.[60] Because of "domestic and other reasons" Crane was unable to speak that year, but she was given an opportunity to speak at the next congress, in August, 1905, in Grand Rapids, Michigan.[61] That year Charles Edward Russell with whom Crane had worked at the *Minneapolis Tribune*, wrote "The Greatest Trust in the World," which began serialization in *Everybody's*. Russell's series of eight articles told how the packers were raising prices despite the declining value of beef cattle and were, at the same time, illegally accumulating millions through rebates disguised as private railroad car charges.[62] In July, 1905, his story prompted the indictment of several beef trust leaders for conspiracy to restrain trade. Plugging into the popular cause of the time, Crane entitled her speech to the butchers and packers, "Shall the Local Butcher Work for Meat Inspection or for the Beef Trust?" She argued that local butchers should organize in each community and build small, up-to-date slaughterhouses. She said they should insist that licenses be required in order to protect themselves from unscrupulous members of the trade, and that they should ask for municipal inspections of meat as rigid as federal inspection.[63] Her speech maintained that the greatest asset to the large commercial packer was the federal inspection stamp, and that the smaller butchers and packers needed a similar system, which would allow them to be competitive. After her address Crane fielded several questions, and her speech was published later in *The Butchers' and Packers' Gazette*.

NOTES

[1]Caroline Bartlett Crane, "Interest in Meat Inspection," unpublished typescript, ca. 1909, p. 1, Crane Papers.

[2]Caroline Bartlett Crane, "The Local Slaughter-house Meat Inspection," Michigan State Board of Health, *Teachers' Sanitary Bulletin* 6 (February 1903): 9–10.

[3]"The Local Slaughter-house Meat Inspection, p. 10; and "Foul Places," *Kalamazoo Evening Telegraph* (25 March 1902).

[4]Crane, "The Local Slaughter-house and Meat Inspection," pp. 10–11.

[5]"The Local Slaughter-house and Meat Inspection," p. 10.

[6]Crane, "The Local Slaughter-house and Meat Inspection," p. 13; and Crane, "Interest in Meat Inspection," p. 3.

[7]"Foul Places," *Kalamazoo Evening Telegraph* (25 March 1902); and "Filthy Beyond Description," *Kalamazoo Morning Gazette-News* (27 October 1903).

[8]Crane, "Interest in Meat Inspection," pp. 4–5.

[9]Crane, Interest in Meat Inspection," pp. 5–6; "Club Women Ask Ordinance," unidentified Kalamazoo newspaper, undated, Crane Papers; and "On Record For Meat Inspection," *Kalamazoo Evening Telegraph* (27 October 1903).

[10]Caroline Bartlett Crane, "Meat Inspection: The Paramount Issue Among Women of Kalamazoo," an open letter published in the *Kalamazoo Evening Telegraph,* undated, Crane Papers.

[11]Crane, "The Local Slaughter-House and Meat Inspection," p. 14; and "Inspection of Meat and Milk Urged by City Council by Mrs. Bartlett Crane," *Kalamazoo Morning Gazette-News* (1 April 1902).

[12]Crane, "The Local Slaughter-house and Meat Inspection," pp. 14–15; and Crane, "Interest in Meat Inspection," pp. 6–7.

[13]Crane, "Interest in Meat Inspection," pp. 6–7.

[14]Crane, "Interest in Meat Inspection," pp. 8–11.

[15]Crane, "The Local Slaughter-house and Meat Inspection," p. 1; and Crane, "Interest in Meat Inspection," p. 11.

[16] Crane, "Interest in Meat Inspection," pp. 12–13.

[17]Crane, "Interest in Meat Inspection," pp. 12–13; "Success in Getting Bill Passed," *Grand Rapids Herald* (30 April 1903); and "Mrs. Crane Wins Out," inidentified newspaper (1 May 1903), Crane Papers; Michigan Legislature, An Act to Provide for the Inspection of Animals Intended for Meat Supplies, *Public Acts, 1903, Regular Session, 1903*, Act 120, pp. 140–43.

[18]Crane, "Interest in Meat Inspection," p. 13; and Michigan Legislature, An Act to Amend an Act to Reincorporate the City of Kalamazoo, *Local Acts 1903, Regular Session 1903,* Local Act 492, Sec. 35, p. 591.

[19] "Warmly Approved by Aldermen," *Saginaw News* (22 September 1903).

[20]Crane, "Interest in Meat Inspection," pp. 15–16.

[21]Ibid.; "Woman's Fury," *Detroit News* (1 December 1903); and "Hearty Talk Before Common Council," unidentified newspaper, undated, Crane Papers.

[22]"Sick Meat Exhibited at the Meeting of Health Officials," *Kalamazoo Evening Telegraph* (11 January 1904); Crane, "The Local Slaughter-house and Meat Inspection," pp. 9–12; and invitation for "Conference of Health Officials in Michigan," January 7–8, 1904, at Ann Arbor, Michigan.

[23]Caroline Bartlett Crane, "Almshouses," 1934 typescript recollections, pp. 1–2; and Caroline Bartlett Crane, "The Need of Nurses at Our County Farms," a speech reprinted from the Michigan State Conference of Charities and Corrections, *Proceedings of the Twenty-Second Annual Convention of the Michigan State Conference of Charities and Corrections*, 1903 (Lansing: State of Michigan Printers, 1904), Crane Papers.

[24]Crane, "Almshouses," 1934 typescript recollections, p. 4; and Caroline Bartlett Crane, "Our Problems of the Poorhouse," *The Commons* (April 1905): pp. 4–5.

[25]Superintendents of the Poor, *32nd Annual Abstract of the Reports of the Superintendents of the Poor in the State of Michigan.*

[26]Crane, "The Need of Nurses at Our County Farms."

[27]Caroline Bartlett Crane, "Women's Clubs as Related to Penal and Pauper Problems," speech reprinted from Convention of the Michigan State Conference of Charities and Corrections, *Proceedings of the Twenty-Third Annual Convention of the Michigan State Conference of Charities and Corrections,* 1904 (Lansing, State of Michigan Printers, 1904), pp. 61–65, Crane Papers.

[28]Crane, "Our Problems of the Poorhouses," p. 7.

[29]Suellen M. Hoy, "Municipal Housekeeping: The Role of Women in Improving Urban Sanitation Practices," in *Pollution and Reform in American Cities 1870–1930,* pp. 174–78.

[30]Caroline Bartlett Crane, "The Women's Civic Improvement League of Kalamazoo, Michigan," pamphlet published 21 April 1906 by the WCIL, Crane Papers; and Lydia G. Wood, "History of Civic League," unpublished typescript, 1914, Crane Papers, p. 1.

[31]Crane, "The Women's Civic Improvement League of Kalamazoo, Michigan," p. 1.

[32]Caroline Bartlett Crane, "Father O'Brien," in 1934 typescript recollections, Crane Papers; "Michigan Catholic Assails Mrs. Crane," unidentified Kalamazoo newspaper, undated, Crane Papers; "Mrs. Crane Replies to the Augustinian," *Kalamazoo Evening Press* (1 May 1910).

[33]Caroline Bartlett Crane, "Visiting Nurse in a Small City," *Charities and the Commons* 16 (7 April 1906): p. 26.

[34]Crane, "Visiting Nurse in a Small City," p. 26.

35Crane, "Visiting Nurse in a Small City," p. 27.

36Helen Christine Bennett, "Caroline Bartlett Crane of Kalamazoo: The First Municipal Expert of America," *Pictorial Review* (September 1910): p. 13; and Mabel Potter Daggett, "One Woman's Civic Service," *Delineator* 73 (June 1955): p. 768.

37"To Beautify Kalamazoo," *Kalamazoo Gazette* (2 April 1904).

38Caroline Bartlett Crane, "The Work for Clean Streets," *The Woman's Forum* (September 1905); "Michigan Women Are Making A Spotless Town," *New York Herald* (8 May 1904); "Women Clean City—Kalamazoo Treated to Spring Cleaning," *Chicago Chronicle* (8 May 1904); "Project Begins," *Kalamazoo Evening Telegraph* (2 May 1904); "Factors of the Street Cleaning Problem," *American City* 6 (June 1912), pp. 895–97; and "Improving Kalamazoo," *World's Work* 20 (June 1910), pp. 13089–90.

39Crane, "The Work for Clean Streets," 4; and Martin V. Melosi, "Refuse Pollution and Municipal Reform: The Waste Problem in America 1880–1897" in *Pollution and Reform in American Cities, 1870–1930*, pp. 115–17; and Charles N. Glaab and A. Theodore Brown, *A History of Urban America* (New York: The Macmillan Company, 1967), p. 178.

40Crane, "The Work for Clean Streets," pp. 4–5.

41Crane, "The Work for Clean Streets," p. 5.

42Caroline Bartlett Crane, "Municipal Housekeeping," speech delivered at Baltimore, Maryland, City-Wide Congress, March 8–10, 1911, reprint from *Proceedings of Baltimore City-Wide Congress*, p. 216, Crane Papers; and Caroline Bartlett Crane, "Clean Streets—How" *Woman Citizen* 8 (8 March 1924): pp. 11–12.

43Caroline Bartlett Crane, "Clean Streets for Chicago" printed pamphlet of address delivered in Fullerton Hall, Art Institute, Chicago, 10 November 1907, at a mass meeting of seventeen men's and women's clubs of the city, printed by the Neighborhood Center Committee of the Chicago Women's Club; and "Report of

Mrs. Crane: Facts about Street Cleaning," *Kalamazoo Evening Telegraph* (29 June 1904).

[44]"Report of Mrs. Crane: Facts about Street Cleaning."

[45]Crane, "The Work for Clean Streets," pp. 8–9.

[46]Crane, "Clean Streets for Chicago."

[47]Neil H. Brennan, "Kalamazoo Civic Improvement League," typescript of academic paper by Western Michigan University student, Charles Starring Papers, Western Michigan University Archives, p. 4.

[48]Crane, "The Women's Civic Improvement League of Kalamazoo, Michigan," Crane Papers, p. 3.

[49]"Comstock's On the Map," *Kalamazoo Evening Telegraph* (12 April 1907).

[50]Crane, "The Women's Civic Improvement League of Kalamazoo, Michigan," p. 3.

[51]Crane, "The Women's Civic Improvement League of Kalamazoo, Michigan," p. 3.

[52]Mabel Potter Daggett, "One Woman's Service in Kalamazoo," pp. 767–68.

[53]Daggett, "One Woman's Service in Kalamazoo," pp. 767–68; and Caroline Bartlett Crane to E. A. Handy, 7 December 1906, Crane Papers. (Handy was president of the Lake Shore & Michigan Southern Railroad. In the letter, Handy is advised that the Michigan State Conference of Charities and Corrections has approved a resolution seeking cooperation with the railroads in "stamping out the tramp evil.")

[54]Clark A. Chambers, *Paul U. Kellogg and The Survey* (Minneapolis: University of Minnesota Press, 1971), pp. 16–38; "Dr. Adler's Great Work," *Kalamazoo Evening Telegraph* (11 March 1905).

[55]"On Methods of Charity," unidentified Kalamazoo newspaper, undated, Crane Papers.

[56]"Dr. Adler's Great Work."

[57]"On Work Among the Children," unidentified Kalamazoo newspaper, undated, Crane Papers.

[58]Neil H. Brennan, "Kalamazoo Civic Improvement League," p. 13; See *Who's Who in America*, s. v. "Caroline Bartlett Crane," 1934–35 ed., vol. 18, p. 626; *Cyclopedia of American Biography,* s. v. "Caroline Bartlett Crane," 1916 ed., Vol. 15, pp. 64–65; Augustus Warren Crane to Caroline Bartlett Crane, 20 November 1908; and Peter J. Schmitt, "Call of the Wild: The Arcadia Myth in Urban America 1900–1930," Ph.D. Diss., at University of Minnesota, 24 June 1966, p. 139.

[59]"Ladies' Lunch in Abattoir," *Kalamazoo Evening Telegraph* (12 December 1905).

[60]"Will Address International Butcher Congress," *The Butchers' and Packers' Gazette* (23 April 1904).

[61]John H. Schofield (secretary of the Master Butcher's Association of America) to Caroline Bartlett Crane, 29 June 1904, Crane Papers.

[62]Charles Edward Russell, "The Greatest Trust in the World," *Everybody's* 7 (May 1905): pp. 147–56, and following numbers.

[63]Caroline Bartlett Crane, "Shall the Local Butcher Work for Meat Inspection or for the Beef Trust," *The Butchers' and Packers' Gazette* 98 (19 August 1905): pp. 1–2.

REFORMISM EXPANDS

Crane's leadership in local municipal housekeeping crusades inevitably led her to involvement in state and national campaigns to improve society. In 1906 her activism encompassed meat inspection, divorce law reform, and a campaign to improve health care for poorhouse patients that would begin in Michigan and extend to the national level.

Early in the year, Crane read an article published in the prestigious medical journal *London Lancet* by meat inspection expert Dr. Adolph Smith that was critical of American inspection standards.[1] She also obtained a copy of a German publication by Robert V. Ostertag entitled *Text-book on Meat Inspection* that found fault with the American system. The federal inspection system as Crane had seen it work in Chicago no longer appeared adequate, though it was still better than any local system. Her reading told her that in the United States, slaughterhouses removed localized diseased meat from a carcass and sold it as being of the same quality as disease-free meat. In Germany animals with localized disease were offered for human consumption, but the public was clearly advised that the meat was of lower quality.

It was Ostertag's criticism that caused Crane to embark on a careful study of federal inspection standards.[2] Crane found that federal regulations, dated June 27, 1904, listed twenty-six diseases and/or conditions for which animals were to be "rejected and condemned."[3] At first she took that to mean that the meat of animals affected with these diseases was excluded from the marketplace; later she confessed that she had not taken the time when she first received it to read the document thoroughly. If she had, Crane would have learned that the section on rejection and condemnation of diseased livestock applied only to animals examined by the packer, before purchase and slaughter, a rule that protected the packer not the consumer, from risk. After slaughter, if "localized" disease was found, meat from other parts of the animal could still be given the Department's stamp of approval. In short, various degrees of disease were allowed in thc carcass and approved for food.

As soon as she made this discovery she went to Chicago to meet with the chief federal inspector, O. E. Dyson, who assured her that the practice was "all right." According to Crane, the inspector said that, for example, after a butcher had killed and dressed a tubercular cow or hog, taken out the viscera, and peeled away the tubercular deposits, he would defy a meat dealer or anyone else to detect a carcass infected with tuberculosis bacilli.[4] Tuberculosis was the most common disease found by meat inspectors, and Crane found it difficult to stomach the fact that packers and inspectors saw no problem in giving the government stamp of approval to diseased flesh.

By the time Upton Sinclair's novel *The Jungle* was published Crane was convinced that the federal meat inspection system was seriously flawed. After it had been refused by several publishers, Sinclair's book was printed in February 1906 by Doubleday, Page, and Company.[5] The dozen or so pages giving gruesome details about meat production immediately drew the public's attention. According to Sinclair, rats, refuse, and even employees were ground into beef products. An immediate clamor for reform began. At the same time, the Pure Food Bill—the

primary legislative issue of the Consumer's League and Dr.
Harvey W. Wiley, chief chemist of the Department of Agriculture—was floundering in Congress. Sinclair's book swept that
proposal out of committee, giving the entire pure food issue new
life. The Pure Food Bill was concerned primarily with chemical
food additives and prohibiting patent-medicine quackery, which
Wiley had devoted much of his life to fighting.[6] After Sinclair's
exposé, letters demanding action flooded President Theodore
Roosevelt's office. Agriculture Secretary James Wilson pleaded
with Roosevelt that the Department was powerless under the
current law.[7] In response to the public outcry, Roosevelt
appointed James B. Reynolds and Charles P. Neill, both New York
social workers, to form a commission to investigate Sinclair's
charges.[8] Meanwhile, with President Roosevelt's approval, Senator
Albert J. Beveridge of Indiana introduced the Meat Inspection
Amendment on May 22. Because of the lack of support from
conservatives, Roosevelt released the report by Reynolds and Neill
on June 4.[9] Their report confirmed Sinclair's charges and added
more fuel to the growing outcry for congressional action.

Because both the Pure Food Bill and the Meat Inspection
Amendment dealt with the purity of foodstuffs, they were
considered parts of the same issue by the public. The two bills
were connected in the public mind because the meat packing
industry used some of the same harmful chemicals as those
employed by the patent medicine and food industries. Four days
after the report of the Neill-Reynolds Commission, Crane spoke
before the General Federation of Women's Clubs meeting in St.
Paul. She bypassed an opportunity to jump on the bandwagon
and praise the federal reforms. Instead, she kept to her pre-
announced topic of "Local Meat Inspection," in which she
condemned the filthy small slaughterhouses that marketed meat

locally and were not subject to federal rules. Before the month was out, both the Pure Food Act and the Meat Inspection Amendment were passed and signed into law by Roosevelt. Meanwhile, Crane wrote to Jacob Riis, asking if it were possible for him to bring the need for local meat inspection to the attention of the president. Riis sent her letter to the president's private secretary, but from there it did not go to Roosevelt as she had hoped but to Reynolds, his commissioner.[10]

In response to Crane's letter Reynolds stated that he agreed that national legislation should control local meat inspection. He also requested a copy of the Michigan Meat Inspection Act, which Crane sent him. On August 2, Crane received a copy of the proposed federal regulations and a letter from Reynolds asking her to critique them.[11] Crane was shocked to find that the new standards were to a large degree identical to the ineffective 1904 regulations. A few days later, Crane rushed to her father's bedside in Keokuk, where he died on August 14 at the age of eighty-one. Upon her return to Kalamazoo, Crane dropped all other work and spent every available moment studying the proposed federal standards. With the help of her husband, who assisted in interpreting the more difficult medical passages, she prepared a twenty-three page typewritten critique, which was submitted to Reynolds on September 24.[12]

In her criticism Crane said that the vital matter in any meat inspection regulations was the set of standards used in determining the fitness of animals at the time of slaughter. "This was practically untouched in the public excitement and discussion which preceded the passage of the new meat inspection amend-ment and the drafting of the new regulations . . . ," she said.[13] Crane added that it was regrettable that the reforms instituted by the government were not accompanied by a revision and elevation of health standards by which the meat is judged, particularly the standards concerning animals infected with bovine tuberculosis.[14] Crane feared the general public would feel a false sense of security because of the alleged reforms. "I feel a far greater sense of danger than ever before, on account of the incompetence of inspectors now employed . . . ," she added.[15]

Crane received no immediate response from Reynolds. The Consumers' League had been active in the passage of the Pure Food laws. On October 20, 1906, Crane received a letter from Florence Kelley, general secretary of the organization, advising her that Reynolds had been asked by President Roosevelt to name a committee to suggest measures for the improved enforcement of the new meat inspection act and the food and drugs act. Crane was to be one of five members of the committee. Crane had been active in Consumers' League affairs and served as a member of the national food inspection committee.[16] Finally, in November, Crane received a letter from Reynolds advising her that he had sent her criticism to the Department of Agriculture, but he had received no reply.[17]

In the fall, Crane met with Alice Lakey, chairwoman of the food investigatory committee of the Consumers' League, and attended league committee meetings on food and the special Reynolds committee to which she had been appointed. In a letter to her husband, Crane revealed her dislike for Lakey:

> I think I have never met anyone so eaten up with self-conceit as Miss Alice Lakey, chairman of the food investigating committee, . . . and her silly old father. It is simply nauseating. I think I will resign from her committee for she tries to pump me, and I'm perfectly sure she will use me to the limit and represent the work as her own wherever she can.[18]

Crane said that Lakey "takes practically the sole credit for the passage of the Pure Food Bill, and tells me how [sanitation reformer] Ellen Richards and others have tried to steal her thunder."

In New York City, Crane met with Reynolds. "I need expect nothing from Mr. Reynolds," she wrote Warren, "about getting my criticism to headquarters [Roosevelt]." She added, however, that Reynolds was anxious for her to remain on the meat inspection regulation committee.[19] After learning that Reynolds was not to be counted on to assist her, she decided to write Secretary of Agriculture James Wilson and pose several questions. In his response, Wilson admitted that 35%—about six billion pounds—of the meat consumed by Americans would not be inspected by the federal service.[20] He defended the new regulations, claiming the "most eminent pathologists, both medical and veterinary, in this country" had approved them, but he refused to name the medical experts.[21] A year later, *New York Herald* investigators said they found conditions in the packing industry as bad as ever.[22] While the public believed that the cleanliness of the meat packing plants was the number-one problem, the experts, including Crane, knew different. The hygiene of meat itself had always been the primary concern of the scientists and of the Bureau of Animal Industry, and the most threatening meat hygiene problem was tuberculosis.

Dr. A. D. Melvin, head of the Bureau of Animal Industry, was fully aware of the economic impact of meat hygiene, and he advised Wilson's special commission of scientific experts on this issue. "I am informed that the losses of one of the largest firms alone amount to $600,000 a year, principally on account of this disease [tuberculosis]," he said. "The condemnation and destruction of such an amount of food means much to the owners, who are usually innocent purchasers and do not receive any remuneration. . . ."[23] In 1906, 13,500 cattle and 95,000 hogs infected with tuberculosis were condemned by inspectors. At the turn of the century, it was not uncommon for as many as 20% of meat animals inspected to be infected.24

Crane had failed in her attempt to influence the new enforcement regulations. During the next two years, however, she would continue researching, writing, and speaking on the evils of the system that failed to inspect 35% of the meat consumed by Americans and gave federal approval to what she considered diseased meat.

Cleaning up the nation's meat supply was not Crane's only concern in 1906. She was also a delegate to the National Divorce Congress. Pennsylvania Governor Samuel W. Pennypacker obtained the cooperation of other governors in calling on Congress to draft a national divorce law. Forty-two of the forty-five states sent delegates; Governor Fred M. Warner appointed Crane and two judges as Michigan's delegates to the congress. Crane was one of only seven women among the more than two hundred delegates, and the only woman delegate from a state east of the Mississippi River.25

The congress's main task was to draft a law that would define common grounds for divorce and recommend a solution to the problems of migratory divorce. The law defined migratory divorces as obtained by a couple married in a state different from the one in which the divorce was sought. During floor debate at the opening session Crane sparked the Congress's first controversy, opposing a resolution that would have greatly restricted migratory divorce. The resolution mandated that the courts in a migratory state recognize only the reasons for divorce allowed in the state where the marriage occurred.26 Although she lost her battle over migratory divorce, Crane felt she had been successful at last in forcing the Catholic chairman of the resolutions committee to hand down a resolution listing grounds for divorce.

In later debate she voiced her criticism of the Catholic chairman and of delegates who she claimed were trying to unduly influence and control the congress's actions. In an interview in the *Washington Post,* Crane said she did not believe that great obstacles should be placed in the way of people who have "good moral ground" for divorce. Divorce, she added, is a great evil, but an "evil made necessary by mistaken conditions."[27]

After the congress Republican President Theodore Roosevelt held a reception in the East Room of the White House for delegates. Crane, who considered herself a Republican and Roosevelt supporter, was less than impressed with the president. She wrote her husband:

> When I was introduced to President Roosevelt as "Mrs. Crane of Michigan," he said, "Oh! indeed! I am so pleased to meet you!" in an oily, nasty voice, and with an exaggerated cordiality in smile and manner that I detest in anybody.

She continued:

> I watched him with others, and I must say I think it would be far better if he did the thing in a frankly perfunctory manner without any pretense of being "so pleased" or "delighted." If all I knew of President Roosevelt were what I saw this afternoon, I should have anything but a favorable impression. Poor man! He is probably dead tired of it all, and I am sorry for him. I made up my mind I would not try to speak a word, for I saw no good in it, and it is a mercy to him to help him through with it as quickly as possible.[28]

The delegates were unable to resolve all the issues at the Washington meeting, so a second session was held in Philadelphia in March,[29] when the congress was able to complete a revised Divorce Code that was recommended to the states for their approval. "The code to which the congress has given its seal of approval is good, and its goodness is chiefly due to the Pennsylvania delegation . . . ," Crane said.[30] She was not optimistic that many states would approve the code, however, and she believed that the greatest good to come from the meetings was the general discussion aroused among the public.

Shortly after the Philadelphia session, Crane and the WCIL Charity Organization came under fire for allegedly supporting easy divorces. The *Detroit Free-Press* reported—and it was copied widely—that the WCIL was engaged in securing divorces for women who contended that their husbands were "burdensome."[31] Crane denied the charge, explaining that the WCIL tried to persuade "burdensome and shiftless" husbands to perform their family responsibilities. She said that the WCIL Legal Aid Committee had provided its assistance in obtaining divorces for women who were abandoned and treated cruelly. In affirming the traditional male and female roles, she said "Our chief work is to strengthen the marital tie; to help men to be good husbands and fathers, and women to be good wives and mothers; to safeguard the financial, social and moral interests of the home."[32] Crane believed that if the man earned the family's income, his wife should provide him with a "full dinner-pail." Many wives were workers at the city's 150 small factories and lacked housekeeping and cooking skills. To train these women, the WCIL hired a visiting housekeeper to provide lessons in cooking and housekeeping. One of the most successful projects of the Charity Organization was a series of conferences between city and county officials and charity workers upon such topics as vagrancy, the non-supporting husband, homeless and neglected children, the elderly and sick, the promotion of thrift, municipal health problems affecting charity, and the bread-winning mother.[33] Charitable relief should be provided women who were struggling to be both mother and bread-winner, Crane argued. A study by the organization's office found that 16% of the persons asking relief were women who had been deserted by their husbands. Crane promptly advised the prosecuting attorney of desertion cases. At least two "struggling widows" were given small stipends by the WCIL. In each case, a child had been compelled to leave school to help in the support of a large family. The stipend given each woman was equal to the amount of money the child earned, and this allowing the child to return to school. Crane said that, if the WCIL budget permitted, additional funds would have been awarded in similar cases.[34] Each of the Charity Organization cases was investigated to determine need. In the course of these investigations Crane discovered that loan sharks in the city charged interest as high as 10% a month on small loans to the poor. She undertook a careful investigation of 250 cases and gave the results of her study to the WCIL officers, who endorsed her suggestion that the problem be brought before the Commercial Club (an organization of businessmen similar to the contemporary Chamber of Commerce).[35] A joint committee of the two organizations was formed to study the issue.

Believing that thrift was one of the best weapons against the loan shark evil, Crane convinced the Kalamazoo Savings Banks to pay a collector to make house-to-house collections of small savings from those not in the habit of saving. During the first eighteen months of the program, a total of $14,500 was placed in four hundred savings accounts. The collector, who made weekly rounds, accepted deposits as small as five cents.[36]

The end of 1906 saw Crane devoted to yet another cause. In December, she presided over the State Board of Charities and Corrections annual convention in Kalamazoo, and under her leadership a joint committee of the Michigan State Federation of

Women's Clubs and of the Michigan State Nurses' Association was formed.[37] Acting on behalf of the joint committee, Crane presented another plan to the Charities and Corrections Convention. The plan called for the Women's Clubs to target poorhouses that either were in great need of a nurse or amenable to hiring a nurse. In cases where the Board of Supervisors would not consent to hiring a nurse because of cost, the federation committee would endeavor to raise enough funds to install a nurse for a few months or a year, hoping that county officials would see the need for the service and assume the cost.

Appointment and supervision of the nurse would be the duties of the state nurses' association. In addition, poorhouses would be systematically visited by local committees of women appointed by the county federation of clubs.[38] Crane said that her proposal, which received support from the State Board of Charities and Corrections, called for two changes in state law: one that required modification of current law to make women eligible for appointment to boards of management for poorhouses, and another that created a system of county boards of charities and corrections, with one-half of the members being women. These boards would work under the State Board of Charities and Corrections.[39] Crane had encountered state restrictions against women serving in governmental positions earlier. In 1899 she had been appointed to the board of directors of the Kalamazoo State Asylum; however, the appointment had to be withdrawn by reform Governor Hazen Pingree because state law forbade women to serve on the board.[40]

On May 16, 1907, in Richmond, Virginia, Crane presented the Michigan plan to the Nurses' Associated Alumnae of the United States, the nation's largest professional nursing organization, and asked its help in making her proposal a national plan. By

14.

A Savings' Collector takes a small deposit from a woman during
the collector's regular rounds. Under Crane's guidance, the
Women's Civic Improvement League initiated a savings
program to fight loan sharking among the poor in the city.

a unanimous vote, the organization approved Crane's ideas and said it would seek the cooperation of its individual state organizations in making her plan a reality.[41] In addition, Crane was asked to act in an advisory capacity to a committee named to implement the strategy. It is important to note that Crane's address gained the support of Miss L. L. Dock of the Henry Street Nurses' Settlement, New York City's best-known settlement. The daughter of a University of Michigan medical professor, Dock was a prominent health reformer during the Progressive Era.

Through her work with the State Board of Charities and Corrections, Crane was named as an honorary member of a legislative committee that drafted a bill to create juvenile courts in Michigan. The bill, which was enacted in 1907, moved jurisdiction over juveniles from circuit courts to probate courts. Crane said that the purpose of the law was to remove

> the child entirely from the category of criminals. It does not punish him for one specific act, but finds out about his environment, natural tendencies, seeking to prevent him from becoming a criminal. Very often it is not necessary to take him from his home. The probation officer looks after him and he is watched besides by the judge, his parents, the schools and truant officer. In most cases, he is saved. [42]

Crane praised features of the law that made juvenile court proceedings confidential and made parents and guardians directly responsible for the child becoming a criminal.

While 1906 was productive on many fronts, it was the year 1907 that would afford her a special niche as a reformer.

NOTES

[1]Crane cites the influence of the *London Lancet* in "Interest in Meat Inspection," p. 25; Louis Filler, *Crusaders for American Liberalism*, New Edition (Yellow Springs, Ohio: The Antioch Press, 1950), pp. 159–70, provides a complete explanation of the circumstances surrounding the growing interest in meat inspection in the United States.

[2]Crane, "Interest in Meat Inspection," p. 25; Robert V. Ostertag's textbook on meat inspection achieved at least nine editions in Germany and four in English, according to the editor's preface to the 1934 American Edition: Robert V. Ostertag, *Textbook on Meat Inspection*, ed. T. Dunlop Young, translated by C. F. Marshall (Chicago: Alex Eger, 1934), p. v.

[3]Crane "Interest in Meat Inspection," p. 27; and U.S. Department of Agriculture, *Rules and Regulations for Inspection of Livestock and Their Products*, June 27, 1904 (Washington: Government Printing Office, 1904).

[4]Crane, "Interest in Meat Inspection," p. 27, and U.S. Department of Agriculture, *Rules and Regulations for the Inspection of Livestock and Their Products*.

[5]Upton Sinclair, *The Jungle* (New York: Doubleday, Page and Company, 1906), pp. 32–45. (Chapter 3 contains the material vividly describing the sickening conditions in the packing houses.)

[6]Filler, *Crusaders for American Liberalism*, pp. 167–68.

[7]U. S. Department of Agriculture, *The Federal Meat-Inspection Service,* published originally as the *Annual Report of the Bureau of Animal Industry for 1906* and issued on February 28, 1908, as a pamphlet for general circulation as cited in Caroline Bartlett Crane, "History of Meat Inspection," unpublished manuscript, p. 127, Crane Papers.

[8]Filler, *Crusaders for American Liberalism*, p. 166.

[9]Filler, *Crusaders for American Liberalism*, p. 167.

[10]James B. Reynolds to Caroline Bartlett Crane, 5 June 1906, Crane Papers. (Reynolds advised Crane that her letter to Riis had been forwarded by President Roosevelt's secretary to Reynolds.)

[11]James B. Reynolds to Caroline Bartlett Crane, 2 August 1906, Crane Papers.

[12]Caroline Bartlett Crane, "Criticism on New Regulations Governing Meat Inspection," unpublished typescript manuscript, Crane Papers.

[13]Crane, "Criticism on New Regulations Governing Meat Inspection," p. 1.

[14]Crane, "Criticism on New Regulations Governing Meat Inspection," p. 4.

[15]Crane, "Criticism on New Regulations Governing Meat Inspection," p. 17.

[16]Florence Kelley to Caroline Bartlett Crane, 20 October 1906, Crane Papers.

[17]James B. Reynolds to Caroline Bartlett Crane, 5 November 1906, Crane Papers.

[18]Caroline Bartlett Crane to Augustus Warren Crane, 16 November 1906, Crane Papers.

[19]Caroline Bartlett Crane to Augustus Warren Crane, 16 November 1906, Crane Papers.

[20]James Wilson (Secretary of Agriculture) to Caroline Bartlett Crane, 14 December 1906, Crane Papers.

[21]James Wilson to Caroline Bartlett Crane, 14 December 1906, Crane Papers. (The Department in 1907 identified the experts on its panel and issued a report entitled *Report of A Commission on Certain Features of the Federal Meat-Inspection Regulations*. A reprint of the report for the Twenty-Fourth Annual Report of the Bureau of Animal Industry [1907] is in the Crane Papers.)

22Upton Sinclair, *The Brass Check: A Study of American Journalism* (Pasadena, California: published by Upton Sinclair, 1920), pp. 50–52.

23U. S. Department of Agriculture, *Report of a Commission on Certain Features of the Federal Meat-Inspection Regulations* reprinted from the *Twenty-fourth Annual Report of the Bureau of Animal Industry* (1907) (Washington: Government Printing Office, 1909), pp. 364–65.

24Interview with Clarence H. Pals, who was director of the Federal Meat Inspection Service, 1960–65, Arlington, VA, telephone interview, 7 September 1985.

25National Congress on Uniform Divorce Laws, *Proceedings of the National Congress on Uniform Divorce Laws*, Washington, D.C., 19 February 1906, pp. 4–8; and "Divorce Delegates Are All Born Fighters," *Washington Post* (21 February 1906).

26National Congress on Uniform Divorce Laws, *Proceedings of the National Congress on Uniform Divorce Laws*, pp. 71–72, 78; and "Tight Nuptial Knot," *Washington Post* (21 February 1906).

27"Womanly Impressions of the Discussion of Divorce," *Washington Post* (21 February 1906).

28Caroline Bartlett Crane to Augustus Warren Crane, 20 February 1906, Crane Papers.

29National Congress of Uniform Divorce Laws, *Proceedings of the Adjourned Meeting of the National Congress on Uniform Divorce Laws,* Philadelphia, PA, 13 November 1906.

30National Congress of Uniform Divorce Laws, *Proceedings of the Adjourned Meeting of the National Congress on Uniform Divorce Laws*, p. 17.

31"Secures Divorces for Women Who Haven't Money to Do It," *Detroit Free Press* (11 March 1906); Crane, "The Women's Civic Improvement League of Kalamazoo, Michigan."

[32]Crane, "The Women's Civic Improvement League of Kalamazoo, Michigan."

[33]Crane, "The Women's Civic Improvement League of Kalamazoo, Michigan."

[34]"The Charities Organization of Kalamazoo, Michigan," pamphlet published by the Charities Organization Department of the Women's Civic Improvement League, Kalamazoo, Michigan, 1 December 1907, Crane Papers.

[35]Crane, "The Women's Civic Improvement League of Kalamazoo, Michigan"; and "Strong Organizations Aim Death-Blow at Loan Sharks," undated Kalamazoo newspaper clipping, Crane Papers.

[36]Daggett, "One Woman's Civic Service," p. 768.

[37]Convention of the Michigan State Conference of Charities and Corrections, *Proceedings of the Twenty-Fifth Annual Convention of the Michigan State Conference of Charities and Corrections and of the County Agents' Association, Kalamazoo, Michigan, December 5–7, 1906* (Lansing, Michigan: State of Michigan Printers, 1907), pp. 1–2, Crane Papers; and Caroline Bartlett Crane, "Report of Committee on Almshouse Reform," *Michigan Club Bulletin* 2 (15 April 1908), pp. 8–13, Crane Papers. (The magazine was the State GFWC official organ.)

[38]State Conference of Charities and Corrections and the County Agent's Association, *Proceedings of Twenty-Fifth Annual Convention of the Michigan State Conference of Charities and Corrections and of the County Agents' Association*, "Plan of Work for the Improvement of Our Michigan Almshouses," by Caroline Bartlett Crane (Lansing, MI: State of Michigan Printers, 1907).

[39]"Plan of Work for the Improvement of Our Michigan Almshouses," by Caroline Bartlett Crane.

[40]Augustus Warren Crane to Hazen S. Pingree, 3 March 1899, Crane Papers.

[41]Caroline Bartlett Crane, "Almshouse Nursing: The Human Need; the Professional Opportunity," address before the Nurses' Associated Alumnae of the United States at Richmond, VA, 16 May 1907, reprinted in *American Journal of*

Nursing (August 1907): pp. 873–80, reprint in the Crane Papers; and "Adopts Scheme of Kalamazoo Woman," *Kalamazoo Gazette* (17 May 1907).

[42]"Michigan System Best in World," *Kalamazoo Evening Telegraph,* undated, Crane Papers; "Spoke on Juvenile Court," undated Kalamazoo newspaper clipping, Crane Papers; and "Analyzes Rival Bills," unidentified Kalamazoo newspaper, undated, Crane Papers.

A MINISTER TO CITIES

In 1907, Dr. J. N. MacCormack, executive officer of the Kentucky State Board of Health and lecturer for the American Medical Association, spoke on public health to the Kalamazoo Academy of Medicine.[1] Crane, who was in the audience with her husband, was asked to speak extemporaneously on public health investigations she had made in Kalamazoo. MacCormack was impressed. Immediately after the meeting he asked Crane to come to Kentucky to perform a statewide public health survey sponsored by the State Board of Health. She declined because she felt the task surpassed her expertise, but, in time, MacCormack's request stimulated Crane to become a municipal sanitation consultant. Crane, who earlier that year had made investigations in the small Michigan town of Hastings, began to consider the possibility of future civic reform crusades. On November 10 she addressed a mass meeting in the interest of "A Better Chicago" sponsored by seventeen of the city's men's and women's clubs. The report of her speech, "Clean Streets in Chicago," was page one, column one news in the next day's *Chicago Tribune*.[2] Crane talked about how the alleys, vacant lots, and streets of Kalamazoo had been cleaned and urged Chicago to use the Waring Street Cleaning System. But, more important, she based her speech on personal observations made of the city. "I made a most interesting tour of the city yesterday morning; was so glad I did it for it helped me so much to say the helpful thing," she wrote in a letter to Warren.

161

In her speech, she reported to her husband, she was careful not to offend political factions:

> I did speak of the same streets, same dirt, and same lack of continuity and efficiency in public work here as at home, but I was careful to say it was not a matter of any particular party or individual so much as because both parties chose street commissioners and not for their fitness to clean streets, but because of their political affiliations.[3]

Before Crane spoke Jane Addams, the founder of settlement work in Chicago, gave her a tour of the Henry Booth Settlement and showed her new buildings belonging to Hull House.

Although her lecture in Chicago was well received, Crane said that she would be more than willing to switch places with a young woman she encountered at a reception with a four-month-old child. "If I had that baby to nurse at my breast, I'd let Alma [the mother] do the lecturing this afternoon," she wrote her husband.

Crane continued her crusades for poorhouse reform and improved meat hygiene. She continued to research meat inspection history and offered to write a history of meat inspection for *Collier's* magazine. Editor Richard Jones rejected the idea, saying that the subject of meat inspection "seems to me . . . largely a matter for legislation rather than public appeal."[4] In June, Crane's inspection of a poorhouse in Fargo, North Dakota, resulted in a new infirmary with adequate medical care for patients.[5] From January to March of the following year she spent most of her time trying to persuade the Kalamazoo County Board of Supervisors to institute reforms at the local poorhouse. Crane, who had never fully relinquished her five-year crusade to improve conditions at the poorhouse, said she again found unacceptable conditions there. She led a citizens' committee on an investigatory tour of the poorhouse[6] and then asked county officials to improve medical care, ventilation, cleanliness, and fire safety. She also asked the group to institute religious services for the inmates and funeral services for the deceased, to adopt legal and humane rules and regulations for operation of the facility, to prohibit the admission of child inmates, and to investigate the poorhouse's management and accounts. But again, the Board of Supervisors refused to act on Crane's requests, claiming that conditions at the facility were excellent.

In March 1908, Crane spoke to the Michigan State Federated Women's Clubs on progress on poorhouse reform made by the Women's Club/Nurses' Committee and on the results of her efforts to improve conditions for the poor in Muskegon two years earlier. She reported that the county commissioners had constructed a poorhouse with a small hospital facility, but had not hired a nurse. In Adrian, however, she said county officials had hired a nurse for the poorhouse, mainly because of the work of leaders of the women's club there. Crane also reported that Miss L. L. Dock, chairman of the National Nurses' Committee formed in Richmond, Virginia, in 1907, had enlisted the cooperation of nurses' organizations in sixteen states to work with the General Federation of Women's Clubs in the formation of committees to urge county officials to hire nurses for health care at poorhouses.[7] Later that month Crane gave an address at the Abraham Lincoln Centre in Chicago on "The Forgotten People," in which she outlined the Michigan plan, which called for county officials and GFWC local clubs to work together to staff poorhouses in each county with a nurse. She reported that she had met with the president of the Illinois State Federation of Nurses, who expressed interest in the plan.[8]

In April 1908 Crane investigated conditions in New Hampshire's corrections facilities and institutions for the poor. She told the New Hampshire State Conference of Charities and Corrections that it should not be proud of having sixteen orphanages because the worst thing possible for a child is institutional life. She was especially critical of the New Hampshire Reformatory for children, calling it a "sore spot."[9] She condemned its use of child labor: "Must you set those little children, some of them not more than eight years old, to making hosiery amid deafening, clanging machinery with the fluff and dust of the wool and cotton flying through the air?" she asked. In lieu of the factory, she suggested that a system of manual training allowing an "outlet for individuality" be instituted.

Letters from Warren again reveal both his loneliness and his penchant for praising her. "The people of New Hampshire are using you as a civilizing agent . . . when you get through with the East and the West, then come home and civilize the savage, who loves you in the primeval [sic] way," Warren wrote.[10]

Crane made a three-day inspection of Calumet, Michigan, in May. As a result of her recommendations, street cleaning in the city was improved, two parks were constructed the next year, additional streets were paved, the public library was improved, and a local charity organization was created.[11] After her investigation in Calumet she traveled west to Kansas City, Missouri, to investigate conditions at the slaughterhouses there. "I have read all the meat inspection documents I intended to read and feel quite prepared for my visit to the Kansas City Abattoirs," she wrote in a letter to her husband as her train neared the city. "I am more and more astounded at the deception practiced on the public. There are three plants I want especially to see in Kansas City."[12] She does not provide any specifics of her investigation there.

Crane returned to Illinois in October speaking to the Illinois State Federation of Women's Clubs annual convention in East St. Louis.[13] In mid-November she made another long train trip alone—this time to Pittsburgh for the national American Civic Association Convention, where she would be named a member of the organization's executive board.

On her trips from home, Crane frequently complained about the use of tobacco. During one of the dinner meetings in Pittsburgh, cigars were given to each male guest. She wrote Warren, "as soon as they began to smoke them I got up quietly and left." She added, "It seems to me an outrage to invite women and then compel them to sit through . . . such misery."[14] From Pittsburgh, Crane traveled to Erie, Pennsylvania, for her first complete out-of-state sanitary and sociologic survey—as she called it.

Crane's investigative technique was based on the model of the sociological survey, except that it stressed critical examination of municipal services and hygiene. Pioneer sociologists had popularized the use of the survey in studying cities. The most prominent American sociological survey had been conducted by Paul Kellogg of *The Survey* in Pittsburgh.[15] Such sociologists as Albion Small and Charles Henderson, under whom Crane had studied at the University of Chicago, believed that information gained in a survey could be used in formulating reform measures. Crane called herself a "municipal sanitarian," a municipal housekeeping "profession" she practically invented. Her profession, however, should not be confused with sanitarians-—sanitation experts who served municipalities. Her method of investigation was a systematic, but personal observation of the water supplies, sewers, street sanitation, garbage collection and disposal, milk and meat supplies, bakeries, food factories, schoolhouses, poorhouses, hospitals, prisons and jails, and institutions of detention for the poor, elderly, orphans, and the mentally ill.[16]

She required community-wide support for her work prior to her arrival for a survey. Although support from women's organizations was always available, at times she demanded wider endorsement. In a letter to the president of the Minnesota Federated Women's Clubs, Isabell Higbee, she said she was "alarmed at the exclusively feminine aspect" of the endorsements for her proposed statewide survey there. Most commonly, sponsors were local or state boards of health, city officials, women's clubs, chambers of commerce, associations of physicians, and civic-minded community groups. In Saginaw, Michigan, Crane was invited by twenty-two organizations to make a survey. She was usually paid $100 per day for single-city surveys that usually lasted three to four days. She received as much as $1,500 for each of her three statewide surveys.[17]

Before visiting a city, she required that a list of eighty-two "Questions About Your City" be answered. She wanted to know about the city's form of government, population, property valuation, tax rate, system of accounting, bond issues for public improvements, water sources and treatment, miles of streets and sewers, methods of collecting refuse, smoke abatement, locations of city parks, playgrounds, schools, and recreational areas. She also requested copies of municipal ordinances concerning meat, milk, and market inspections. In addition, she asked that the city's daily newspapers be mailed to her for several months before her visit. By the time she entered a city Crane had remarkable knowledge of its government and community affairs.[18]

Although she usually insisted on secrecy prior to her arrival, once she arrived the publicity was highly organized, as a long trail of reporters followed her from place to place, usually in several cars. Her earlier work as a journalist was useful in her survey work. On most occasions, she had a press release that she had written ready to give to reporters.[19] Her talent as a public speaker also was useful, as she usually made several speeches in a city, including an address at a mass rally at the conclusion of her survey, where she revealed her findings. Crane asked that her sponsors provide the "largest and best place" possible for this meeting. On several occasions, she stressed her conviction that civic improvements could best be made when partisan politics was removed from municipal government. Mayors and aldermen, she said, should be elected on the basis of their ability to manage a city's affairs, and a city's medical officers and street commissioners should be chosen based on their ability, not on their party affiliations. Several communities also commissioned Crane to put her findings into writing so they could be published and used as "the bible" of civic reform by city and state officials.

Before Crane started a survey she was usually sworn in as a local or state health official, to give her findings official sanction and to protect her from lawsuits. While making her surveys she was accompanied by community officials and important persons, including, if possible, the wife of the mayor, thus giving her work even further official sanction. Several of the local officials usually assisted her by being volunteer note-takers.

In Erie, Crane said she found a "bad municipal government," but she received support from the local newspaper. She told Warren that she believed that a juvenile she had discovered in the city jail would be removed soon, that the school system was the real weakness of the city, and that a total of nine-hundred persons had come to hear her speech at the conclusion of her three-day study.[20]

Warren shared Caroline's interest in public health and sanitation, he frequently wrote to her about his work. When Crane was in Erie, for example, Warren was preparing for an x-ray exhibit in New York City. His letters contain several references to efforts to improve his x-ray technique, which was considered one of the best in the nation.[21] Her letters also showed an intense interest in her husband's work. She said that when she returned from Erie, she would

> sit before the fire and talk and talk and you will hold me and there love, and then you will hold me some more, and then we will go into the office and you should show me all the things you have been doing.[22]

The Brown Thrush continued to be their trysting place. Caroline wrote: "O, darling, if only the weather will last till I get home; if only! So we can fly to our trysting place and be alone in the peace and sanctity of the Little Brown Thrush."[23] Caroline's public life apparently enhanced Warren's interest in her sexuality. He found it exciting that she was at one moment a "sweet charming woman who plays the piano and washes her dishes" and when the telephone rings "she is transformed into another—a woman of power. I love them both. The visions fuse."[24]

Warren and Caroline were together only briefly when she returned from Pennsylvania; Warren left for New York City to present his exhibit to the American Medical Association in December, and shortly after his return, she boarded a train for Daytona, Florida, where she would make another survey. While Crane was in Daytona the mayor of the nearby town of Sea Breeze asked her to conduct an informal survey.[25] In Sea Breeze, Crane noticed that the Hotel Clarenden had no fire escapes. The mayor defended the building, telling Crane that the fire department had a "remarkable water supply." It was not until later that

To

Him

"On the Eve of the New Year"

1906

15.

A photo of "Him" (A. W. Crane) taken from a page in *At the
Brown Thrush* written and compiled by Caroline Bartlett Crane
as a gift to her husband (from the collection of Crane's
grandaughter, Julie Durham).

'Twas a Sunday afternoon,
I well remember, in the
middle of August; and 'twas
my birthday. Smiling, He left
me for perhaps ten minutes,
then returned to say that the
two trees were mine and the
fulness thereof, which I
interpreted as meaning the
fair and wooded stretch
of summer-land around
and between. This was my
lovely birthday present from
dear Him, and when the
deed was duly made and
delivered to Brother Taylor,
I fancied myright there

16.

A text page from *At the Brown Thrush.*

Crane learned that the mayor was the sole owner of the hotel. He refused to respond to her request for action to correct the hotel's deficiency, telling her to tend to her own business. She did: the very next day she reported the incident to the State Fire Department. About two weeks later a fire destroyed the hotel. Fortunately, no one was killed, but several guests had to jump from windows to safety.

From Daytona, Crane traveled to Wilkes-Barre, Pennsylvania, where she performed another survey. In both Wilkes-Barre and Daytona she founded women's civic leagues similar to the WCIL in Kalamazoo.

Crane faced the first serious objection to her investigations in Scranton, Pennsylvania, where she performed a survey in March. After an uneventful day, citizens asked her to visit the community's new Hillside Home, which served as a combination poorhouse, orphanage, and insane asylum for the city of 130,000.[26] Because the building was new, several officials apparently expected her commendation. She entered a clean-looking room and asked that a patient's feet be uncovered. The citizens accompanying Crane turned their heads when the patient's feet were exposed: they were filthy and covered with sores. On the evening before her inspection she obtained building plans of the institution and, the following day, asked to see rooms that were not on the tour officials had carefully planned for her. By the time she left the building her escorts were uneasy. The following evening at a public meeting at the Paoli Theater, she condemned the facility because it had only one physician and one trained nurse for the poorhouse population of 440 persons, among whom were included many sick, elderly, and insane patients. In addition, she said that the patients should be segregated by the nature of their mental disease and that a ward for patients with tuberculosis should be established. The citizens of the city applauded Crane's findings, but the Poor Board, which administered the facility, was outraged, and it gained the support of the mayor. Crane had been staying in the home of the mayor and his wife, who was the president of the Civic Improvement League that had invited her to the city.

The attack against Crane was vicious. A newspaper sided with the Poor Board and in an editorial attacked her role as a reformer, claiming that being "a professional fault finder" (Crane received $300 for the survey) required no skills.[27] The editorial writer added:

> Poor soul, if she were only a man in place of a He female, one could go hammer and tongs after her, in a good old-fashioned way, proving conclusively that she is simply in a business for what she can get out of it. . . .

In contrast, another newspaper editor in Scranton called Crane a "civic revivalist" and contended she was the "foremost civic reformer in America." During a subsequent speech, Crane defended herself and her role in the city. "What am I here for?" she asked. "You did not ask me to make a social call."[28] Crane wrote Warren that she was "indignant" about the criticism of her work and that she had packed her trunk and was ready to leave.

In Scranton she created another sensation by breaking a school firebox. The result was outright panic. The teachers did not know how to handle the situation, and the children were confused. When the teachers discovered that the alarm was a drill they were highly indignant and protested that the children had not had time to put on their coats. The school administration said that no fire drills had ever been held in the winter because it was too cold.[29] In addition to school fire safety problems and the inadequacies of the Hillside Home, Crane made some unfavorable comments about several other aspects of the community. As soon as she left, all the politicians—who had run for cover while she was there—came out of hiding and loudly denied her charges.

Crane's reputation as a consultant continued to grow, however, and in May of 1909 she succumbed to MacCormack's persistent request to investigate social and sanitary conditions in Kentucky cities. Crane's visit was sponsored by the State Federation of Women's Clubs, the State Health Board, and several local associations of physicians. During her six-week stay she inspected sanitary conditions in twelve cities: Cynthiana, Lexington, Richmond, Frankfort, Harrodsburg, Shelbyville, Louisville, Bowling Green, Paducah, Henderson, Owensboro, and Hawesville.[30]

While Crane found support for her work, opposition existed in Kentucky as well. In Harrodsburg, for instance, she inspected a poorhouse and suggested in a speech that the physician who had been hired to provide medical care had been professionally incompetent in allowing such deplorable conditions to exist. The physician sued Crane for libel, seeking $1,985 in damages.[31] Fortunately, the State Board of Health stood by Crane and the physician later dropped the suit. The episode in Harrodsburg had an even happier ending for the poor and elderly when a new poorhouse was constructed as a result of her investigation.[32]

Crane's work was well received in Louisville. On her first day there she visited the county poorhouse and spoke to a crowd of five hundred. On the following morning, she visited slaughter-houses with a state veterinarian and city health officer, and in the afternoon she investigated jails and black settlement work. Within twenty-four hours after she had inspected and condemned the poorhouse in Louisville, a county official called a special session of his fiscal court to appropriate money for reforms there.[33]

In Henderson, Crane found it unbelievable that one intersection could hold a school and three saloons.[34] She was also critical of the city's hospital: "You have a city hospital that isn't worthy of the name," she said in a public speech, "and I wouldn't go there for treatment if I had my consciousness."[35] Claiming that the operating room was filthy, she pleaded with officials to place administration of the hospital in qualified hands. Nurses at the hospital responded angrily in a newspaper article the next day. "They just ought to do with that Mrs. Crane in Henderson the way they did with her in Paducah—just run her out of town," said the nurse in charge.[36]

Crane's observations were not confined only to municipal sanitation. She lectured on the advantages of a centralized charity organization and frequently took time to mention a community's moral sins. In Bowling Green, she discovered a house of prostitution "at the city's gate by the railway station."[37] She visited the brothel with a local social worker and found a two-week-old baby and a fifteen-year-old girl who was working as a prostitute. Crane made an issue of the house, and after she left a grand jury closed the establishment. Before she left the state, Crane inspected the state's prison and its School for the Feeble Minded. On both occasions, she was accompanied by the governor.[38]

The six weeks in Kentucky turned out to be a very arduous time for Crane. She wrote to Warren that she would never leave home for such a prolonged period again because it had been such a "great strain on my heart-strings, even if not on my heart." She said she longed to "elope as was our custom for the secret peace and deliciousness of the Brown Thrush nest."[39] Another letter written by Caroline in Kentucky revealed how close she and Warren were in their professional lives as well. She gave Warren credit for many of the ideas behind her work: "It is wonderful and oh! it hurts me to be appreciated and applauded because of my gift for popular expression, for the very ideas and dreams that often you have begotten in me."[40] By mid-June Crane had completed her survey, with the final stop in Hawesville, where her mother's relatives resided. "My people are such nice people and so highly thought of, and it warms my heart to be with my mother's kin," she wrote to Warren.[41]

Crane's investigations in Kentucky resulted in several other achievements. In Frankfort prominent citizens called a meeting a week following her survey to organize an effort to make possible several reforms Crane had suggested, and her investigation in Paducah resulted in the construction of a new tuberculosis sanitarium. Overall, her trip was so successful that it resulted in the legislature's approval of a bill requiring tubercular tests for dairy cattle and improvement in the handling of milk supplies.[42]

Crane made her final Kentucky report to the State Federation of Women's Clubs meeting in Owensboro.[43] In addition, the August 1909 issue of the *Kentucky Medical Journal* was devoted to details of her work and included excerpts from several newspaper editorials that both praised her work and urged solutions for the state's numerous public health problems.[44] Calling Crane an "apostle of civic righteousness," the *Lexington Herald* said: "It would be well for Kentucky if she were paid a salary by the State to visit every county and tell the result of her observation."[45] Like a revivalist, she had led a public crusade throughout the state, arousing interest in many cities for reform of sanitary conditions.

NOTES

[1]Caroline Bartlett Crane, "Sanitary Survey," in typescript recollections, p. 1, Crane Papers; and Crane, "The Story and the Results," Crane Papers.

[2]"Cleaner Chicago Prospect Bright," *Chicago Tribune* (11 November 1907).

[3]Caroline Bartlett Crane to Augustus Warren Crane, 11 November 1907, Crane Papers.

[4]Richard Jones to Caroline Bartlett Crane, 4 January 1907, Crane Papers.

[5]See Helen Christine Bennett, "Caroline Bartlett Crane," in *American Women in Civic Work* (New York: Dodd, Mead and Company, 1915), p. 40; "The Stormy Petrel of Slothful Cities," *The North American Magazine* (a newspaper feature syndication), Philadelphia, Pennsylvania, 12 December 1909; and Caroline Bartlett Crane to Augustus Warren Crane, 5 June 1907, Crane Papers.

[6]"How Row is Growing Out of Inquiry," *Kalamazoo Gazette* (25 January 1908); "Will Issue No Call for Special Session," *Kalamazoo Gazette* (28 January 1908); "Civilization is Insulted by Koster," *Kalamazoo Gazette* (2 February 1908).

[7]"Report of Committee on Almshouse Reform," *Michigan Club Bulletin* 2 (15 April 1908), pp. 8, 12, 13.

[8]Caroline Bartlett Crane, "The Forgotten People," an address given at the Abraham Lincoln Centre, Chicago, 24 May 1908, to the Illinois Federation of Nurses and published in *The Quarterly of the Illinois State Association of Graduate Nurses*, reprint in the Crane Papers.

[9]Caroline Bartlett Crane, "Address before New Hampshire State Conference of Charities and Corrections," speech delivered May 1, 1908, pamphlet published by the New Hampshire Conference of Charities and Corrections, Crane Papers; and "The Sore Spot of New Hampshire," *Portsmouth* (New Hampshire) *Herald* (1 May 1908).

[10]Augustus Warren Crane to Caroline Bartlett Crane, 1 May 1908, Crane Papers.

11"What Mrs. Crane Did in Calumet in Three Days," *Kalamazoo Evening Telegraph*, undated, Crane Papers; and Caroline Bartlett Crane to Augustus Warren Crane, 13 May 1908, Crane Papers.

12Caroline Bartlett Crane to Augustus Warren Crane, 23 May 1908, Crane Papers.

13Caroline Bartlett Crane to Augustus Warren Crane, 19 October 1908, Crane Papers; "The White Woman's Burden," address given to the Illinois Federation of Women's Clubs at its annual convention in 1908 as printed in an undated publication entitled *Illustrated Review*.

14Caroline Bartlett Crane to Augustus Warren Crane, 18 November 1908, Crane Papers.

15Martin Bulmer, *The Chicago School of Sociology* (Chicago: University of Chicago Press, 1984), pp. 66–67.

16Caroline Bartlett Crane, "Questions About Your City," unpublished typescript questionnaire that was sent to cities to be surveyed, Crane Papers.

17Caroline Bartlett Crane, "City Sanitarian," unpublished draft of a description of her occupation as city sanitarian, p. 4, Crane Papers.

18Bennett, "Caroline Bartlett Crane," in *American Women in Civic Work*, pp. 22–24.

19Bennett, "Caroline Bartlett Crane," in *American Women in Civic Work*, pp. 24–26.

20Caroline Bartlett Crane to Augustus Warren Crane, 24 November 1908, Crane Papers.

21Augustus Warren Crane to Caroline Bartlett Crane, 20 November 1908, Crane Papers.

22Caroline Bartlett Crane to Augustus Warren Crane, 23 November 1908, Crane Papers.

[23]Caroline Bartlett Crane to Augustus Warren Crane, 24 November 1908, Crane Papers.

[24]Augustus Warren Crane to Caroline Bartlett Crane, 17 November 1908, Crane papers.

[25]See "For Civic Improvement," *Halifax* (Daytona, Florida) *Journal* (20 January 1909); Helen Christine Bennett, "Caroline Bartlett Crane," in *American Women in Civic Work*, p. 40; Helen Christine Bennett, "Cleaning Up the American City," *The American Magazine* 76 (September 1913), p. 48; Caroline Bartlett Crane to Augustus Warren Crane, 13 January 1909, Crane Papers; and Caroline Bartlett Crane, "Sanitary Surveys," in Recollections, Crane Papers.

[26]"Mrs. Crane Scorns Treatment of Insane at Hillside Home," *The Scranton* (PA) *Republican* (8 March 1909); Caroline Bartlett Crane to Augustus Warren Crane, 3 March 1909, Crane Papers.

[27]"Mrs. Crane Reformer and Lecturer," *The Scrantonian* (14 March 1909).

[28]Helen Christine Bennett, "Caroline Bartlett Crane of Kalamazoo: The First Municipal Expert of America," *Pictorial Review* (September 1910), p. 13.

[29]Helen Christine Bennett, "Caroline Bartlett Crane of Kalamazoo: The First Municipal Expert of America," p. 13.

[30]See "Mrs. Crane's Work in Kentucky," *Kentucky Medical Journal* 7 (1 August 1909), pp. 600–04; Caroline Bartlett Crane, "Sanitary Surveys," in typescript recollections, pp. 3–4; and "Biographical Sketch," p. 10, Crane Papers.

[31]"Warm Roast for Harrodsburg by Mrs. Bartlett Crane," *Harrodsburg Republican*, undated, Crane Papers; "Damage Suit Filed Against Mrs. Bartlett Crane," *Harrodsburg Democrat,* undated, Crane Papers; William W. Stephenson to Mrs. Caroline Bartlett Crane, 28 May 1909, Crane Papers. (The letter is from an attorney representing Dr. Witherspoon, who was allegedly libeled); Caroline Bartlett Crane to Augustus Warren Crane, 29 May 1909 and 2 June 1909, Crane Papers.

[32]Bennett, "Cleaning Up the American City," p. 48.

[33]"Mrs. Crane's Work in Kentucky," pp. 600–04.

[34]"Mrs. Crane Scolds a Little, Praises a Great Deal and Admits That She Is Shocked," unidentified Henderson, Kentucky, newspaper, undated, Crane Papers.

[35]Bennett, "Caroline Bartlett Crane of Kalamazoo: The First Municipal Expert of America," p. 63; and "Angry Nurses: Pyrotechnic Explosion of Bottled Wrath at City Hospital," *Henderson* (KY) *Journal,* undated, Crane Papers.

[36]"Angry Nurses: Pyrotechnic Explosion of Bottled Wrath at City Hospital," *Henderson* (KY) *Journal,* undated, Crane Papers.

[37]Caroline Bartlett Crane to Augustus Warren Crane, 3 June 1909, Crane Papers.

[38]Crane, "Sanitary Surveys," in typescript recollections, p. 4, Crane Papers.

[39]Caroline Bartlett Crane to Augustus Warren Crane, 4 June 1909, Crane Papers.

[40]Caroline Bartlett Crane to Augustus Warren Crane, 12 June 1909, Crane Papers.

[41]Caroline Bartlett Crane to Augustus Warren Crane, 13 June 1909, Crane Papers.

[42]See "Mrs. Crane's Work in Kentucky," pp. 600–04; Alan S. Brown, "Caroline Bartlett Crane and Urban Reform," *Michigan History Magazine* (Winter 1972), p. 299; and Bennett, "Caroline Bartlett Crane of Kalamazoo: The First Municipal Expert of America," 63.

[43]"Mrs. Crane's Work in Kentucky," p. 600.

[44]"Mrs. Crane's Work in Kentucky," pp. 600–04.

[45]*Lexington Herald,* cited in "Mrs. Crane's Work in Kentucky," p. 601.

AMERICA'S HOUSEKEEPER

Although she was active on many fronts during this period, Crane never lost interest in meat inspection reform. On October 15, 1909, she toured Chicago meat-packing plants to see whether the new inspection regulations were being enforced.[1] There she was allowed to see five confidential *Service Announcements,* documents that, in theory, were circulated only to employees of the Bureau of Animal Industry, the agency of the Department of Agriculture that was in charge of meat inspection. She photographed the documents and returned them to their owner, whose identity she promised not to disclose.

The *Service Announcements* were interdepartmental directives on how meat inspectors should interpret and enforce government regulations. Crane discovered that the documents also were provided to meat packers, though she, representing the public, had been denied formal access to their contents. She believed that they revealed a conspiracy among packers and federal inspectors to lower meat inspection standards.[2]

On October 20, Crane revealed her findings in a speech to the American Public Health Association convention in Richmond, Virginia. In her speech entitled "What is Happening to American Meat Inspection?" she spoke of the documents and their sinister purpose. Mr. M. Dorset of the biochemistry division of the Bureau of Animal Industry rose from his chair and interrupted her address, loudly denying that any such documents existed.[3]

181

One of the *Service Announcements*, however, was repro-
duced in *The News Leader*, a Richmond area newspaper, on
October 21, the day when Crane was scheduled to show all the
documents—she had photographed five—to the APHA executive
committee. For some reason, the committee abruptly changed its
mind and refused to allow her to show the documents,[4] and an
Associated Press wire story on October 22 said that the APHA
"had disposed of the sensational charges" and adopted,
unanimously and without debate, a resolution declaring that the
charges had not been sustained.[5]

The action by the APHA was a terrible defeat for Crane,
who felt that she had not been given fair treatment and that the
Department of Agriculture lobby had won the day. In an October
20 letter to Warren, she said the "D. A. man sent here, without
doubt, is trying to crush it [the effort to have a committee
appointed to investigate her charges]." She added, "He tried to
get the reporter not to publish it or send it by Associated Press."[6]

Immediately following her defeat Crane boarded a train to
New York City, where she planned to ask magazine editors to
publish her findings. In a letter written on the train that day, Crane
reported having two visions[7] and confirmed that she had had such
visions regularly for many years. She wrote:

> You know what they are like—very clear and distinct, like
> colorless transparencies, somewhat like the negative of a
> photograph, except that they are not negative and like a
> finished picture in air instead of on a card. And you know I
> never have them except when I am exhausted and that I never
> see anything unpleasant—so that before I knew you, I did not
> discourage them.

In her first vision Crane saw her own face "angelic and glorified—rapt, and uplifted . . . yet it was much more beautiful and young." In the second vision, she saw herself in an old cemetery where tombstones and aged trees were about to fall on her. Interpreting the visions as mystical occurrences, Crane wrote of them as "real experiences of the inner life."

Following the visions, still in a daze, she said she started "spasmodically" to bite her tongue. This happened twice, she said, making her cry in pain. In the same letter she disclosed that she had another "bad habit—which I am going to conquer . . . the horrid tearing at my thumbs when I am nervous." She added:

> My poor right thumb will show to your practiced but sympathetic eye, a great battle field. It is a nasty habit and I've got to break it and I will. But I have to tell about it here, to make an exact record, physical and psychological, of what happened. The right thumb before I left the hotel was swollen and red, but not throbbing and gave me quite some anxiety. I held it for half-an-hour under the hot water faucet, then rubbed away all the abrasion I could, and bound it up with glyclothy. It no longer hurt me by the time I went to bed.

Crane's correspondence reveals much about her personality. She was intelligent and willful, and at the center of her personality was a perfectionistic ethical/religious code that stressed duty. But she also had a darker side. Physicians, psychologists, and historians have attempted to explain the nineteenth-century and early twentieth-century phenomenon of "Women's Diseases." The "Women's Disease Syndrome" was connected closely with yet another mental malady that was not fully understood—hysteria.[8] At that time women were viewed by society as weak, irrational captives of their wombs. Although she was an intelligent, masterful woman, Crane had apparently suffered from a nervous breakdown in 1898. According to a letter written by Warren in 1906, he feared that she would again suffer from "nervous prostrations," a term that also was closely related to hysteria.

In March 1910 Crane traveled to St. Paul, Minnesota, to lecture to a predominately male audience of the Minnesota Conservation Congress.[9] Contemporary society may find it easy to dismiss the importance of Crane's accomplishments, but a newspaper report of her appearance at the congress sheds light on the difficulties she faced because of gender bias. "It was amusing to watch the faces of some of the delegates yesterday when the women appeared as speakers," a *St. Paul Pioneer Dispatch* reporter noted. Crane was introduced by Isabell Higbee, president of the Minnesota General Federation of Women's Clubs; the reporter continued:

> Some of the delegates gasped when they saw a woman arise and speak extemporaneously with such ease and grace. One man in the front row was considerably amused; it was evidently a funny thing to him to see a woman talk to men! He shook with mirth several times and evidently enjoyed it more than a moving picture show. . . . Governor [A. O.] Eberhart applauded Mrs. Crane with the rest. Even he was a little astonished that a woman could make such a speech as she did.

In Minnesota Crane also made a speech that caused a stir back in Kalamazoo, where it was reported that she had been critical of the failure of the Catholic women of Kalamazoo to join in the work of the Women's Civic Improvement League. In defending herself, Crane said that she had only mentioned that the WCIL board did not include Catholic membership, although the league's charity organization had always helped Catholics and

Protestants alike. She did, however, add that she had been met with rudeness from the local Catholic priest when she tried to obtain Catholic involvement in the WCIL.[10]

Crane resumed her work as a municipal sanitation consultant in April, making surveys in Nashville and Chattanooga, Tennessee. The most remarkable event of her trip was an account of her climbing into a steam locomotive engine in Nashville to tell its engineer how to cut down on smoke pollution. In Nashville Crane also formed an anti-smoke league. Soon after completion of her survey there she received a letter from one of the community's women leaders telling her that

> plans are already on foot to clean up and paint the market house and the mayor wishes the city council to appropriate money for a three-storied market house, the two lower stories for produce and the top floor for a public hall. . . . There are also recommendations for flushing the streets two or three times a week.

Crane was to receive similar letters from leaders in other communities she surveyed.[11]

In May, Crane went to New York to talk to the editors of *Everybody's* magazine about the possibility of publishing her work on the history of meat inspection in serial form. Upon arrival, she went to ask Arthur Kellogg, editor of *The Survey*, for advice in dealing with the magazine. But when she talked to *Everybody's* editor, Theodore Drieser, she found that he had lost his former enthusiasm about the serialization of her manuscript, which at the time was incomplete.[12] Crane left New York City without any promises from the magazine and went to Hagerstown, Maryland, to do another survey. In Hagerstown she condemned a school on account of fire risk and other conditions. The school board objected to her criticism, but a grand jury sustained her and closed the school until changes were made.[13]

She later made a return appearance in Erie, where she again urged the city to clean up its water supply. But city officials again failed to act on her advice, and in January 1911 the worst typhoid fever epidemic in years—103 deaths and 946 cases—-broke out in the city of seventy thousand. An editorial entitled "Mrs. Crane Told Us" voiced the city's regret that it had not followed her advice to improve its water supply.[14]

Crane's speech on municipal housekeeping at the Minnesota Conservation Congress was a preview of her work throughout the state that fall. Beginning in September, she spent forty-five days in Minnesota. The work represented her largest state survey and comprised investigations in seventeen cities.[15] The Minnesota GFWC was one of Crane's sponsors in Minnesota, and its conservative nature was revealed in a letter to Crane from Higbee, who expressed her dissatisfaction that suffrage organizations were advertising Crane's plans to survey the state's cities.[16]

One of the most difficult surveys was in Rochester, the site of the Mayo Clinic. She was faced with the sensitive task of telling the Mayo family that the water supply to their hospital was contaminated. She wrote to her husband, "The Mayos, of course, did not want a word to go out against the water, which is used in their great hospital and in all the hotels that house their patients." She added:

> I think also they have stock in the water company. They assure me that experts say it is above all suspicion, but I know better and I know that when I have finished tomorrow night they will know better, if they do not now. The same old cry, "we have never had any typhoid here" is raised here.[17]

Mrs. Charles Mayo accompanied Crane on the inspection tour the next day. During the tour Crane showed Mrs. Mayo that the cement cesspool at the county poorhouse had overflowed into a small stream that emptied into Bear Creek, which supplied the city's water. The situation was made even more difficult because Crane's host in Rochester was a member of the medical staff. Crane did succeed in convincing the Mayos, and at the final rally meeting Dr. Charles Mayo asked the audience to show its thanks with an extra round of applause. After she left Rochester city officials immediately brought the matter to the attention of the county supervisors, who agreed to seal the overflow and empty the cesspool.[18]

Duluth proved to be another difficult survey. There she found terrible low-rent housing and rooming conditions. The Bethel Mission, which provided housing for many of the city's poor, was mismanaged, she said, but her assertion came under attack by defensive city officials. Crane said people tended to assume that they had no housing problem unless tall tenement buildings filled the skylines.[19] Many communities, however, listened to Crane's gospel. In Eveleth her revelations resulted in a new milk inspection ordinance that required testing for tuberculosis, and at Albert Lea city officials were inspired by her investigation to construct a new city hospital.[20]

In Minnesota she inspected fifty school buildings and reported that many were over-crowded, poorly ventilated, and unscientifically lighted. Minnesota, she said, should urge local school officials to provide proper seating for children. She said she saw entire schoolrooms of children who suffered from fatigue because their seats were so high they could not brace their heels on the floor. Crane claimed that dirty, dark school bathrooms, usually located in basements, as well as a shortage of toilet and

17.

Minnesota Governor, A. O. Eberhard, fourth person from left on the front row, poses with Caroline Bartlett Crane, at the Minnesota Conservation Congress in St. Paul in 1910. To Caroline's right is Dr. Harvey Wiley, who was the chief chemist of the U. S. Department of Agriculture.

washing facilities, were to blame for the spread of many contagious diseases.[21]

By November, Crane was beginning to feel the stress of the long Minnesota survey. From St. Paul she wrote that she was "depressed and apprehensive." She said that the papers had given her "good notices and only if I can get hold of myself all ought to go well."[22] Apparently feeling guilty for her prolonged absence from home, she also wrote to Warren that when she returned, she would help him find time for his own scientific experimentation and original work. In letters written a few days later, she again complained of "horrible depression" and promised that she would never again attempt such a long survey.[23]

Newspapers frequently listed Crane's recommendations in bold letters on the front page, as was true of the *Minneapolis Tribune* on November 21, 1910. The front page of her former employer's newspaper read:

> Minneapolis as viewed by Mrs. Crane's eyes:
> Minneapolis has a bad, very bad milk supply.
>
> Minneapolis has a poor and ineffective milk ordinance and the one now before the council is worse.
>
> Minneapolis has the worst high school building in the country for a city of its size.
>
> Minneapolis has no ordinance to prevent the unsanitary handling of food stuffs after they leave the factory or shop.
>
> Minneapolis has poor street car service at the rush hour.
>
> Minneapolis has a poorly ventilated library, a poorly ventilated courthouse, and some of its schoolhouses are poorly ventilated.

Minneapolis has no ordinance to prevent the overworking of girls in department stores.

Minneapolis has a first-class lodging house ordinance and inspection system.

Minneapolis has some very good school buildings.

Minneapolis has good hospitals.

Minneapolis has good streets, boulevards and parks.

Minneapolis has a number of other good things and outside of the first things mentioned, is all right, thank you.[24]

Crane's published report of her work in Minnesota, *Report on a Campaign to Awaken Public Interest in Sanitary and Sociologic Problems in the State of Minnesota*, is the most comprehensive documentation of her sanitary and sociologic survey work. The purpose of the campaign, she said in the introduction to the 224-page volume, was:

to help communities to understand and to improve the material conditions under which the people live; to bring into the public mind the consciousness of the city as the larger home, and to show that sordid and unwholesome conditions of life for even the poorest people should be regarded as something affecting the larger family; that the penalties for neglect of "even the least of these" may fly far to light upon the most prosperous and tenderly guarded home; to teach that we cannot have "city beautiful" until we have the city clean and wholesome; to induce the people to undertake the study of their own problems; to help them to correlate official and unofficial effort, and finally, to leave behind the kind of public sentiment which will enable officials, civic associations, and even individuals to work unafraid for civic health and the general welfare.

(The "City Beautiful Movement" was a utopian, turn-of-the-century movement based on the belief that it was possible to design the perfect city.[25])

In 1911 Crane returned to Louisville, Kentucky, this time as a delegate to the National American Woman's Suffrage Association. Upon her arrival, the newspapers treated her as a conquering heroine and gave her prominence in the press greater than that given Jane Addams and equal to that enjoyed by Anna Howard Shaw, who was by then president of the National American Woman's Suffrage Association, and by Emmeline Pankhurst, the famous radical British suffragette who was a featured speaker. Crane appeared in photographic layouts with Shaw and Pankhurst in both daily newspapers. According to a letter to her husband, the layouts were performed according to explicit instructions of the newspapers. Both newspapers asked for Pankhurst, Shaw, Dr. Harvey Wiley (chief chemist of the Department of Agriculture), and Crane. Addams, who was elected a vice-president of the NAWSA at the convention, was bypassed by the press.[26]

Crane spoke at the NAWSA convention on the necessity of home rule for cities and reiterated her rationale for suffrage: "Politics at its best is a noble profession in which we earnestly desire to engage," she said; "Woman's long experience in homemaking and mothering of children has fitted her for politics just as well as have man's activities in trades fitted him."[27]

Also from Louisville she wrote to her husband that she was unhappy with the bickering among the women. She said that she was "heartsick over the miserable quarrels and jealousies manifested in the convention."[28] Crane had served for several years as a member of the NAWSA executive board.[29]

   In 1911, Crane also made surveys in Rochester, New York; Saginaw, Michigan; and Knoxville, Tennessee; and she addressed the City-Wide Congress on "Municipal Housekeeping" in Baltimore.[30] The congress was held to discuss a wide-ranging agenda of topics on urban problems. While she was in Baltimore she also made a partial survey of the city and organized a Civic Improvement League. (Crane would later claim that she was instrumental in the founding of about twenty or so such leagues.) That same year, she spent ten days in Brooklyn and New York City, lecturing to several groups. Her most prominent appearance was as part of a lecture series for the New York Child Welfare League. The series featured two other lecturers—former President Theodore Roosevelt and Senator Beveridge of Indiana, who had been the main sponsor of the 1906 Meat Inspection Amendment. Crane also addressed the League for Political Action, the Civic Forum, and the Liberal Ministers' Luncheon group. She returned to New York in 1912 and 1913 for lecture appearances before the League for Political Action. In 1912 she spoke on "Some Common Problems of American Cities," and in 1913 the title of her address was "Municipal Efficiency."

   During the 1911 lecture series and on other occasions Crane was the guest of Mrs. Robert G. Ingersoll, the widow of Colonel Ingersoll whose encounter with Crane in 1896 had catapulted her to the status of a national personality. Mrs. Ingersoll's daughter, Mrs. Wallace Hill Brown, was president of the Child Welfare League. Crane was particularly interested in Mrs. Brown's daughter, Eva, who would later publish a collection of Colonel Ingersoll's letters. As usual on her visits to New York, Crane visited with Albert Shaw, environmental reformer and editor of the *Review of Reviews*, and with Arthur Kellogg and Paul Kellogg of *The Survey*. In addition, a dinner was given in her honor by reformer Maud Nathan, president of the Consumers' League.[31]

By 1912, Crane had earned a national reputation as a lecturer and evangelist of civic righteousness. She informed cities about their civic sins and aroused citizens' evangelistic fervor to work for the civic health and general welfare of their communities. In a letter about her survey work to Belle LaFollette, wife of Wisconsin Progressive Senator Robert LaFollette, Crane said she was "first and foremost a preacher—and always shall be."[32]

Crane's most challenging struggle for the civic good occurred in 1912, by which time she had been writing and researching for about five years on her *History of Meat Inspection*. The manuscript had grown to two hundred pages, and traced the history of federal meat inspection from 1879.[33] She described the history as "a chronicle of packing-house statesmanship in Washington; of disingenuousness and trickery towards Europe, and towards American consumers as well. . . ." Crane had not yet convinced a widely circulated national magazine to serialize her manuscript despite expressions of interest and support. Paul and Arthur Kellogg of *The Survey*, for example, offered to publish an article on her research but said that the small size of their journal would not allow them to run a serialized history,[34] and Albert Shaw, editor of the *Review of Reviews*, believed his journal, which was political in nature, was not an appropriate forum for Cranes articles. Shaw, however, did write her letters of introduction and recommendation to other publishers.[35]

Finally, on March 20, *McClure's* magazine informed Crane that it would publish a condensed version of her history in its June issue, only to withdraw the offer a week later. *McClure's* had begun publishing the investigative journalism of the so-called "Muckrakers," Lincoln Steffens, Ida Tarbell, and Ray Stannard Baker in 1903. By 1910, muckraking was becoming less popular, and by 1912, it had almost disappeared.[36] Cameron MacKenzie, the magazine's editor, explained in a letter to Shaw that Crane's story was rejected because he saw it as an attack on the laxness of the USDA instead of, as he had previously thought, an assault on the meat-packing industry. MacKenzie added: "It isn't our policy to go in for 'muckraking' and the public would probably consider such an attack to be 'muckraking'."[37]

After this response from *McClure's,* Crane made arrangements with Republican Progressive Congressman John Nelson of Wisconsin for a congressional hearing. He filed a resolution with the Committee on Expenditures in the Department of Agriculture to ask for an investigation of the department's meat inspection enforcement. The resolution charged both that the USDA had issued secret orders (*Service Announcements*) that "nullified" the 1906 law and regulations and that the department was guilty of violations of federal meat inspection laws and regulations.[38]

Crane checked into the Hotel Driscoll in Washington on April 21, but her appearance before the committee was delayed until early May because of the congressional investigation of the sinking of the Titanic. During the delay she went to Fort Dodge, Iowa, to perform a survey, and examined federal meat inspection techniques in Des Moines, Iowa.[39] When she returned to Washington in early May, a letter from Warren urged her not to put too much faith in Congress. He wrote: "I am very impatient to hear of your adventures in Congressland. You are a 20th century Alice in Topsy-Turvy Land—another name for Congressland.

Congressional investigations may fade like the Cheshire Cat, with only the smile left."[40]

The hearing finally opened May 8, with Crane, the star witness, appearing first. Chairman Ralph W. Moss, an Indiana Republican, began with a reminder that time was a factor as the congressional session was drawing to a close and "we are quite busy."[41] He also warned Congressman Nelson that at any moment the committee might decide to stop taking testimony and close the hearing. Chairman Moss made it clear that the meat inspection proceedings constituted merely a hearing—not an investigation. In order for a full investigation to take place, the committee would have to support Nelson's resolution and then act to schedule the probe and the parameters of the investigation.[42] Because of the attention by the press, much of the public thought that the hearing was a full-blown investigation. Immediately after Nelson filed his resolution, the packers' lobby hurried to Washington, and telegrams from chambers of commerce, banks, and western cattlemen poured in upon members of Congress.[43]

As soon as the hearings started the Department of Agriculture instigated a smear campaign against Crane. In a flier that was sent to the major newspapers and magazines by Solicitor George P. McCabe, the USDA's top legal officer, the USDA implied that Crane inappropriately received money from the National Cash Register Company to make sanitary surveys and to criticize the Department of Agriculture. The flier read, in part:

> . . . Mrs. Caroline Bartlett Crane, who is now under contract to work for the National Cash Register Co., of Dayton, Ohio, at a compensation of $100 per day. Mrs. Crane *has been investigating* the meat-inspection service for some years and it would be interesting to learn *who is paying for her work.* She has traveled extensively and well and the expense

connected therewith has been large. *Who has stood the expense?*[44]

Crane told the committee that these allegations were untrue, that she had been asked to go to Dayton, Ohio, in February, 1912, to survey conditions at the National Cash Register plant, and that for her work she had received her usual consulting fee of $100 per day.[45] In his column in *Good Housekeeping*, Harvey W. Wiley defended Crane and claimed that the USDA's insinuations were untrue: "The official attack upon Mrs. Crane sets a record in official documents which has never before been attempted by any Department of the government," he said. "The statements made in regard to Mrs. Crane are clearly libelous, and had they been made by a private individual, would be actionable in a court of justice."[46]

The flier impugning Crane's integrity was only the first document disseminated by the USDA during the hearings. Daily press releases giving only the department's point of view were mailed using franking privileges or were hand delivered to newspapers by department employees.[47] Twenty department clerks and inspectors attended the hearings daily and applauded, sneered, and laughed in their attempts to harass Crane and the other witnesses. Crane said in a letter to her husband on May 10 that "The Department of Agriculture is terribly scared. About 20 of them, including Melvin, McCabe, Mohler, Bennett, are at every session. The greatest anxiety and alarm is written on their faces."[48]

In her testimony Crane charged that the USDA had issued regulations, *Service Announcements*, and ZY Circular (interdepartmental) letters that violated the original intent of the 1906 law. In particular, she said the 1906 legislation mandated that meat transported between states be hauled in sealed railroad cars and required that each carcass be stamped individually to indicate that it was "sound, healthful, wholesome, and fit for human food." Crane said that 1908 regulations allowed meat-packers to ship meat freely between their plants in unsealed railroad cars. She said a 1907 *Service Announcement* permitted the legend "U. S. Inspected and Passed" to be placed upon canned meat as by the packing companies in violation of the meat inspection law and its regulations. She said that at an "Armour & Company's plant in Chicago one could see thousands of flat pieces of tin already embossed with the government inspection legend, ready to be made into pails." To show that it was child's play for the packing companies to misuse the labels, Crane displayed a pail of lard embossed with the "U. S. Inspected and Passed" legend. It read: "Armour's Simon Pure Leaf Lard, United States Inspected and Passed under the Act of Congress, June 30, 1906, establishment 2-A."[49] She asked the committee to inspect its contents. One member removed the cover and revealed an inner metal cover into which "U. S. Inspected and Passed" had been stamped at the time of manufacture. When this inner cover was removed the committee found not lard but candy, which Crane had placed in the pail.

Crane told the committee that she believed the regulations approved in 1908 established low standards of hygiene. She testified that while the public believed that tubercular animals were passed only if isolated tubercular nodules were found, in actual practice tubercular meat was passed even when lesions were found in several parts of the carcass.[50] USDA figures indicate that about 1% of all meat—by weight—was condemned by inspectors and that 87% of condemned meat was infected with bovine tuberculosis.[51] Furthermore, she maintained that the *Service Announce-*

ments, which she had discovered in 1909, in many cases secretly superseded the intent of the 1906 Meat Inspection Act.[52]

The Bureau of Animal Industry claimed that the *Service Announcements* were merely confidential, "advisory" communications meant only for the eyes of its inspectors, but Crane countered that, in truth, the documents were given to meat packers as well and were denied only to the general public.[53] The *Service Announcements* permitted several unhygienic practices that lowered and violated the standards set by the regulations, she added, in giving the following examples: beef, mutton and pork containing tapeworm eggs were allowed to be passed for human food; tongues that had lumpy jaw sores cut off were sold under federal guarantee; tumorous organs were ordered passed after the tumors were cut off; parasitic intestines were permitted to be used as sausage skins after the worm-nodules were scraped off; and pork infected with cholera was used in canned meat and sausages.[54]

Possibly more secretive than the *Service Announcements* were the "ZY Circulars," which were also denied Crane by the USDA[55] and which could not be found in the Congressional Library. The "ZY Circulars" served a purpose similar to the *Service Announcements*—interpreting regulations and setting new policy. A. D. Melvin, in an interview, said that the Service Announcements were issued as "a confidential publication only during 1907 and 1908." He contended that the documents had been provided to the packers, stockmen, and members of the press beginning in 1909.[56]

Melvin maintained, moreover, that Crane "does not understand many things about the inspection system and the regulations, and anything she does not understand she suspects of being crooked. She has gone out of her way to place a sinister construction upon perfectly innocent things." To counter his comments Wiley, who attended several sessions of the hearings and was on the list of witnesses, said Crane was one of the "highest authorities on meat inspection in the world."[57]

Several times during her testimony Crane stressed that the best American meat was being exported. Foreign countries knew that the United States inspection was not reliable and compelled packers to send them the best meat available.[58] According to her, the first meat inspection law was enacted in 1891 in response to pressure from European countries who wanted assurances of the quality of the American meat they imported, and the United States' regulations still required a higher standard of inspection for exported meat. Under questioning she said she believed that the responsibility for meat inspection should be taken from the USDA and the Bureau of Animal Industry, that the Bureau of Animal Industry was created to promote the meat industry and effective meat inspection would be contrary to that purpose. But she thought that the main problem at the time was the USDA's administrative personnel. She said Wilson, McCabe, and Melvin were in power at the time of the 1906 disclosures, and instead of correcting the problems they had been guilty of lowering the standard of inspection as set forth in the reform law.[59] "It is not a question of animal industry, or animal pathology, but of the public health," she declared:

> I take the side of the people in this matter, and I do not think the people have been properly represented in the questions arising between the packing interests and the experts who have made the rules for the packers' guidance.[60]

Crane added that she had asked S. E. Bennett what effect the new regulations had had, and his reply was: "They have made a good deal of difference. We found we had been throwing good meat into the tanks."[61] Following her testimony, three former government meat inspectors each corroborated her testimony.

The committee adjourned its hearings on May 22. Initially it was reported that the hearings were postponed to give members time to examine testimony, but it seems that politics had more to do with the delay; President Taft was in trouble in his own party, and in the Fall the more liberal Republicans would break from the GOP and support Theodore Roosevelt and the Progressive Party.[62] Crane wrote to her husband that the *New York American* newspaper said the delay "is because the Democrat Committee thinks Nelson is getting too much glory out of it and they want to put it off a little and then take it up on their own motion."[63] Nelson said that the "reason given by the committee for terminating the hearings was that it had to return to the investigation of the Everglades scandal, which had been interrupted by the hearings upon my resolution."[64] Crane, of course, was very much disappointed at the failure to gain a full investigation immediately. Warren urged her to return home, but she stayed in Washington to revise and edit her testimony after discovering several errors in it.[65] The pressure of the hearing and the uncertainty of its outcome caused Crane to despair. She wrote her husband:

> I am simply desperate. I can't get anything done and I walk back and forth on the street unable to control my face and my fears. It is hard that you don't cheer me. I am heartsick and I am in one of those terrible negative phases when I am paralyzed in my effort. I feel more separated from your sympathy than from you. I feel hanging in air.[66]

Crane's attack on the Department of Agriculture would have been a task for anyone, but for a woman it was particularly difficult. Before Crane began her testimony she had sought to establish her credentials by citing a long list of newspaper and magazine articles endorsing her work. Despite her effort, the *New York Times,* which printed six articles about the Nelson Resolution Hearings, did not give any details of her testimony,[67] although it did prominently mention the three former meat inspectors who testified to collaborate her contentions. Furthermore, Crane felt that muckraker Charles Edward Russell, who had been her co-worker at the *Minneapolis Tribune* and who had earned a niche in history books for his 1905 exposé of the corrupt business practices of the meat industry, attempted to steal credit for her investigative work. Crane's contention has merit; in a 2,500-word magazine article that he published after the hearing, Russell mentioned Crane only once—and then only near the end—although nearly the entire article was devoted to her work.[68]

On May 20 Nelson introduced a House Resolution asking for an investigation of government press agent and public relations activities. The Committee on Rules granted an immediate hearing on May 21, which revealed that most of the governmental departments and agencies had hired news release writers. Newspaper correspondents testified that these "agents" were unnecessary and that they were used to suppress information more often than to supply it. They also reported that department news bureaus were used, as was the bureau of the Department of Agriculture in the meat hearing, to mislead and misinform the public, to aggrandize the department officials, and to make political attacks on members of Congress and others who criticized any feature of the administration.[69] Furthermore, violations of printing laws and the franking regulations were shown in the printing and circulating of publications at government expense. The circular that claimed Crane was employed by the National Cash Register Company had been sent out at government expense on the Department of Agriculture's franking privilege. Crane was called as a witness in the press agent hearing and reiterated her denial of the charges made in the circular.[70]

Crane finally realized her work in Washington was finished when the meat inspection hearing did not resume. She was not finished with her fight but returned home and renewed her effort to have her *History of Meat Inspection* published.

While she maneuvered to find a publisher for her findings on meat inspection, Crane found time in 1912 for a sanitary survey in Montgomery, Alabama, and for work on behalf of woman suffrage.

In August and September she worked for a suffrage referendum in Michigan. Republican Governor Chase Osborn endorsed a resolution for a referendum on the constitutional amendment, and it was to be placed on the ballot in the Fall.[71] Anna Howard Shaw, the president of NAWSA, wrote Crane that she was excited when she heard that the referendum was to be voted on. She recommended that the Michigan Equal Suffrage Association call a meeting of supportive organizations such as the women's clubs, Macabees, Granges, and Farmers' Alliance to plan the campaign. "Unfortunately," she continued, "the submission of the amendment in Michigan came so late and was so unexpected that every dollar of the fund in the national treasury had been pledged to other states," though, she added, she had a special fund reserved for the NAWSA president, with which she could provide Michigan some financial support.[72]

Headquarters for the Kalamazoo Suffrage Association was in the *Telegraph-Press* newspaper building. In the hot, stuffy campaign headquarters women dressed in long dresses and high button shoes worked long hours organizing the campaign effort. They campaigned door-to-door and handed out buttons and literature at the factories and on the downtown street corners. The margin of the vote was razor-thin, but when Crane left for a survey in Montgomery she thought that the suffrage referendum had won. The claim to victory was premature. In a controversial recount the anti-suffrage forces were declared victors by 712 votes.[73] The next year another referendum vote was held, and the suffrage forces lost by 100,000 votes, a remarkable change in sentiment.[74]

The survey in Montgomery in November had to be conducted more diplomatically than usual because Crane was a Yankee reformer in the former capital of the confederacy, but she did not hesitate. She amazed her sponsors by starting her survey immediately upon arrival, on the morning of November 12. She did not even check into her hotel room until that evening. Crane was met in Montgomery by writer Christine Bennett Maupin, who planned to pen an eyewitness account of the Montgomery survey for *American Magazine*.[75]

Most frequently Crane's investigations were called sanitary surveys, and news reports of her work stressed municipal sanitation. Maupin's report is significant because it provides an in-depth look at the sociological aspects of Crane's survey work. Crane sought to enlighten the communities she surveyed on social justice issues, and she measured her success by achievements in social reform as well as in municipal sanitation. Her surveys invariably featured investigations of prisons and institutions serving the poor, the mentally ill, and the handicapped.

After inspecting Montgomery's street sanitation, water system, and dairies, Crane asked to see the poorhouse. When she was advised that it was not the property of city government she replied: "Well, it is on city ground and most of the inmates come from the city. I want to see it."

The county poorhouse was in a picturesque location. Crane's car drew up under great trees as the shadows of late afternoon fell. A run-down red brick building stood at one end of the yard and at the side were a number of two-room wooden cottages. The cottage porches were occupied by several men and women. A man slowly walked over to welcome the visitors.

Crane asked if he was the superintendent. "No'm, that is, not exactly. I get'em by contract. I get thirty-seven-and-a-half cents a day from the county for everyone's that's here."

"And for what, what do you do?"

"Do, ma'am?" the superintendent replied. "Why I feed' em, I clothe' em, I bury' em."

Inside the first cottage were two old women, one of whom was blind, and four children, the oldest a girl of thirteen. The poorhouse manager said that the children were there only temporarily. He explained that their mother was ill and in the hospital and their father had disappeared.

"There was no other place in the city to send them," he added. Upstairs in the cottage, the group found several seriously ill patients who were not receiving proper medical care. Several females begged the visitors for cloth to make quilts so they could find relief from their boredom. Crane's group went next to the black section of the institution, which was separated by a board fence from the white section. There lay a bedridden, blind woman. Across the room, her toddler sat on the knee of an elderly woman while an infant lay on a nearby bed. "I've been here three years," said the sick woman. "What is the matter?" Crane asked. The manager told her that the woman had syphilis.

Next on the survey was the city jail which Crane soon discovered was a firetrap. There her entourage discovered three young men, all about twenty years of age, peering through a grate in the door of a windowless cell. Crane noted that the inmates were all standing and did not have any chairs. One inmate contended that if they sat on the floor they would be eaten by rats. The jail keeper denied the charge, but when Crane insisted on going into the cell and pointed her small flashlight into a corner rats scurried away from the beam.

Crane and other members of the group were shocked to find how harshly prisoners who were in jail for minor offenses were treated. All of them were dressed in white striped suits and forced to work on road repair gangs.

Later in the day Crane discovered that she was well-known by most of the city's teachers, several of whom announced their support for her work. The first school Crane visited was in a factory district. The children sat up straight at Crane's request, betraying the fact that many pairs of heels failed to reach the floor, a situation Crane frequently condemned as potentially causing injury. She also told school officials that many windows admitted light at an angle that could damage the children's eyes. In addition, toilets, cellars, and furnaces were inspected, and she made suggestions on how to improve the ventilation and fire protection.

One of the first grade classes, Crane reported, was very large, and she commented on its size to its teachers. "It will be much smaller after tomorrow," the teacher replied. She explained that the compulsory education law required children to be in school only eight weeks. The teacher said that many of the children would return to work in the cotton mills following classes that day.

The children were listening. Crane asked one boy nearby, "And do you go?" He nodded. The teacher said that the boy was the brightest in her class. When questioned by Crane the boy said he earned fifty cents a day at the mill.

Crane dropped to her knees and put her arms around the boy. "Ladies," Crane pleaded, "here is your chance to begin this thing. Fifty cents a day will lift the mortgage from this child's life. His teacher says that of all her boys he is her brightest—her right-hand man. Free him—give him his chance." The tears were running down her cheeks and down the cheeks of the women, while the city commissioner went into the hall to clear his throat. Before the group left the room they pledged to give the boy's parents the equivalent of his wages at the mill.

As usual, at the end of her four-day survey Crane held a mass meeting to announce her findings. She talked for two hours, tactfully presenting her compliments first. Then Crane revealed the conditions at the schools, city jail, and county poorhouse:

> I seem to see those children born under county auspices, going into your schools for their eight weeks of study, sent to your county jail like the little fellow of eleven whom I saw there running about the corridor just outside the pens in which you keep your desperate criminals—because you have no other place for him and he is supposed to have stolen some sacks—sent through the city jail and put in stripes for the first offense, unwanted, unloved, discredited, returning to those pens where now your murderers wait for their day of doom—what else can I see for him?

The following morning Crane left the city. In her four-day survey, she had inspected the waterworks, streets, alleys, sewer system, the incinerator, the poorhouse, two elementary schools for whites, two elementary schools for blacks, a high school for whites, the city slaughterhouse, five dairies, four factories, six bakeries, the city jail, the county jail, the tuberculosis treatment camp, the hospital for contagious diseases, the city laboratory, the free medical dispensary, six meat markets, four restaurants, one cold storage plant, two movie theaters, a railroad station and yard, and a boarding house. She had interviewed several city officials, made a study of the administration of the health department, been interviewed by several reporters, and made seven speeches.

There is no record of Crane's reaction to segregation in Montgomery, although she did make a point of inspecting the black section of the poorhouse and two black schools. She attempted to arrange a meeting with Booker T. Washington, the foremost black leader in America and principal of the Tuskeegee Normal and Industrial Institute in Tuskeegee, Alabama. Washington, however, was out of town during her Alabama visit.

Immediately after her departure a committee was named to make sure the small boy did not go back to the mill, and a campaign was inaugurated to abolish the contract system of operation of the county poorhouse. The campaign also called for a county election to provide funds to erect a new building. Officials discovered that the eleven-year-old mentioned by Crane in her speech had been illegally detained at the jail, and he was admitted to a reformatory. All this happened within one month after Crane's survey—a typical reaction to her gospel of civic righteousness.

Following the Montgomery crusade, Crane attended the 1912 NAWSA Convention in Philadelphia and served as one of the leaders of five large rallies held outside Independence Hall.[76]

Suffrage received another setback in that same month with the defeat of the Progressive Party candidate, Theodore Roosevelt, who promised to continue to support woman's suffrage. Democrat Woodrow Wilson was elected in the three-way race. He also had pledged to support suffrage, and the movement's leaders reminded him of his pledge with a parade on the eve of his inauguration in Washington, on March 4. Crane, who marched in the parade alongside NAWSA President Shaw in the clergy section,[77] said she was "insulted by hoodlums." She added, "Do you know, I don't think as well as I did of men, as a class; I am afraid I rather despise them."

Crane's long struggle to have her views on meat inspection published concluded in March, 1913, when *Pearson's* magazine published the first of a five-article series by Crane entitled "U. S. Inspected and Passed." The editor's note preceding the first article read, in part:

> The editors of three of the leading magazines were eager to publish it [her findings], but later, though, before a page of the story was written, decided that publication was impossible. One of these editors made a contract with Mrs. Crane and paid the price and then, before a page of the story had been written, wrote that he could not publish the story "for reasons which I should be glad to go into verbally." Well, here is the first of Mrs. Crane's stories. It, and those to follow, will tell the whole truth about our meat inspection. Not a single fact will be suppressed. Read and you will know of your betrayal by your own officials in this matter of your and your family's health.[78]

Pearson's was the last haven of muckraking. Arthur West Little, its publisher, was not a muckraker, but he was a firm friend and admirer of them. He had taken over the subscribers' list of the defunct *Hampton's*, and in the April 1912 issue, he announced that *Pearson's* was to be a free organ of opinion and independent of advertising. For this reason, he said, the magazine was dispensing with pictures and would be printed on inexpensive pulp paper. Its one attraction would be its subject matter, and Little was confident that an audience existed for that. "The Magazine Which Prints the Facts That Others Dare Not Print" was its motto.[79]

At that time *Pearson's* circulation was not large enough to rank it as a major magazine; however, muckraker Samuel Hopkins Adams reviewed Crane's articles for *The Survey* magazine,[80] and the review was reprinted in the *General Federation Magazine* in January, 1914.[81] The review advised readers of Crane's accomplishments in the field of meat inspection and listed her main contentions, many of which had first been heard in detail during the Congressional hearing in 1912. In the articles Crane recommended several remedies to improve meat inspection, including stiffening current federal law, compelling correct labeling on the principle of the pure food slogan "Let the label tell," establishing municipally controlled and inspected slaughterhouses, and, wherever practicable, creating municipally owned slaughterhouses.

In his review of Crane's articles Adams said that Crane implied, but did not specify, that the resignation of top Department of Agriculture officials was essential. "James Wilson has resigned," the review said. "George P. McCabe has retired to private life with a stain upon his official record. A. D. Melvin remains at the head of the Bureau of Animal Industry. For the good of the new administration Melvin should be summarily removed."[82]

Crane's views also received support from *LaFollette's Weekly*, which published a lengthy defense of her work and reprinted one of the articles published in *Pearson's*;[83] and for at least two more years Congressman Nelson attempted to get a meat inspection reform bill through Congress. He failed. On April 3, 1913, the City Club of Philadelphia listened as Crane and two federal meat inspection officials debated on the condition of meat inspection in the United States. Crane felt the club's forum was fair, "in marked contrast" to the 1909 hearing before the American Public Health Association.[84] The main points of Crane's meat hygiene crusade were that all meat should be inspected and that meat infected with contagious diseases such as tuberculosis should not be passed on to the consumer. It was a battle Crane could not win. After 1914 Crane's attention turned to other affairs, and it was 1967 before all meat was inspected. The Wholesome Meat Act mandated that meats that did not cross state lines must be inspected by standards at least equal to the federal inspection standards.[85] If states did not meet the standards of the federal meat inspection program, the federal government could assume control of state inspections. In 1972 regulations were finally issued that mandated that any carcass found to be infected with tuberculosis, even locally, could be used only for lard.[86] But by 1972 the condemnation of cattle infected with bovine tuberculosis was no longer an economic issue to the packers, as the disease was a very rare occurrence.

In July, 1913, Crane made her third statewide survey in Washington, where she investigated sanitary and sociological conditions in twelve cities.[87] Within only a few months her lifestyle would change yet again.

NOTES

[1]Crane, "History of Meat Inspection," p. 177; U. S. Department of Agriculture, Bureau of Animal Industry, *Service Announcements,* 16 March 1908, 15 January 1908, 15 October 1908, several undated announcements and photographic copies in Crane Papers; "Documentary Evidence Produced by Mrs. Crane," *The News Leader* (Richmond and Manchester, Va.) (21 October 1909), Crane Papers.

[2]Caroline Bartlett Crane, "What is Happening to American Meat Inspection," unpublished manuscript that purports to be "substances of a paper given before the American Public Health Association," Crane Papers.

[3]"Documentary Evidence Produced by Mrs. Crane," *The News Leader* (21 October 1909).

[4]Caroline Bartlett Crane to Augustus Warren Crane, 21 October 1909.

[5]"Says Mrs. Crane Didn't Prove Her Accusation," *Kalamazoo Evening Telegraph* (22 October 1909). The Associated Press wrote the story.

[6]Caroline Bartlett Crane to Augustus Warren Crane, 21 October 1909.

[7]Caroline Bartlett Crane to Augustus Warren Crane, 22 October 1909.

[8]Carroll Smith-Rosenberg, "The Hysterical Woman: Sex Roles and Role Conflict in Nineteenth-Century America," in *Women's Experience in America: An Historical Anthology*, ed., Esther Katz and Anita Rapone (New Brunswick, Conn.: Transaction Books, 1980), pp. 315–37; Lorna Duffin, "The Conspicuous Consumptive: Woman as an Invalid," in *The Nineteenth Century Woman: Her Cultural and Physical World*, ed., Sara Delamont and Lorna Duffin (London: Croom Helm, 1978), pp. 30–32; and Ann Douglas Wood, "The Fasionable Diseases: Women's Complaints and Their Treatment in Nineteenth-Century America," in *Women and Health in American Historical Readings*, ed. Judith Walter Leavitt (Madison: University of Wisconsin Press, 1984), pp. 222–38.

[9]"Mrs. Crane Opened Eyes of Mere Men," *St. Paul Pioneer Dispatch* (19 March 1910); Bennett, "Caroline Bartlett Crane: The First Municipal Expert of America," p. 63; and Caroline Bartlett Crane, "Women's Stake in Conserva-

tion," *Proceedings of Minnesota Conservation and Agricultural Development Congress* (St. Paul: Minnesota State Board of Immigration, 1910), pp. 151–59.

10"Mrs. Crane Replies to the Augustinian," *Kalamazoo Evening Press* (1 May 1910).

11Caroline Bartlett Crane to Augustus Warren Crane, 23 October 1910, Crane Papers.

12Caroline Bartlett Crane to Augustus Warren Crane, 14 May 1910, Crane Papers.

13"Plain Talk to a City," *Baltimore Sun* (11 May 1910).

14"Mrs. Crane Told Us," *Erie Dispatch* (22 February 1911); and Caroline Bartlett Crane, *General Sanitary Survey of Erie, Pennsylvania, 1911* (Erie, Pennsylvania: n. p., 1911); and Caroline Bartlett Crane, "Sanitary Surveys," in Recollections, pp. 7–8.

15Caroline Bartlett Crane to Augustus Warren Crane, 23 October 1910, Crane Papers.

16Isabell Higbee to Caroline Bartlett Crane, 23 October 1910, Crane Papers.

17Caroline Bartlett Crane to Augustus Warren Crane, 23 October 1910, Crane Papers; and Crane, *Report on a Campaign to Awaken Public Interest in Sanitary and Sociologic Problems in the State of Minnesota* (St. Paul: Minnesota State Board of Health, 1911), p. 21.

18Caroline Bartlett Crane to Augustus Warren Crane, 24 October 1910 (telegram), Crane Papers.

19"County Almshouse a Disgrace," *Duluth* (Minnesota) *Herald* (3 October 1910); and Crane, *Report on a Campaign to Awaken Public Interest in Sanitary and Sociologic Problems in the State of Minnesota*, pp. 179–82.

20Bennett, "Caroline Bartlett Crane," in *American Women in Civic Work*, p. 40.

[21]Crane, *Report on a Campaign to Awaken Public Interest in Sanitary and Sociologic Problems in the State of Minnesota*, pp. 151–76.

[22]Caroline Bartlett Crane to Augustus Warren Crane, 13 November 1910, Crane Papers.

[23]Caroline Bartlett Crane to Augustus Warren Crane, 18 November 1910, Crane Papers.

[24]"Minneapolis Exposed by Sanitation Expert," *Minneapolis Tribune* (21 November 1910).

[25]Maury Klein and Harvey A. Kantor, *Prisoners of Progress: American Industrial Cities 1850–1920* (New York: MacMillan Publishing Co., 1976), pp. 423–24.

[26]*Louisville Herald*, photograph headlined "Four Big Noises Among Suffragists" (23 October 1911); and *Louisville Courier-Journal,* photograph headlined "Prominent Figures" (23 October 1911).

[27]Harper, *The History of Woman Suffrage*, 5: 322.

[28]Caroline Bartlett Crane to Augustus Warren Crane, 21 October 1911, Crane Papers.

[29]*Notable American Women: A Biographical Dictionary*, s. v. "Caroline Bartlett Crane" by Charles Starring; and *Woman's Who's Who of America 1914–1915*, s. v. "Caroline Bartlett Crane" (Reprint ed. by Gale Research Co., Detroit, Michigan, 1976).

[30]Crane, "Municipal Housekeeping," a speech reprinted from Baltimore City-Wide Congress, *Proceedings of Baltimore City-Wide Congress,* March 8–10, 1911 (Baltimore: Baltimore City-Wide Congress, 1911).

[31]"Rev. Caroline Bartlett Crane Receives Signal Honors in East," *Kalamazoo Evening Press*, ca. 1911, Crane Papers; and numerous letters, Crane Papers.

[32]Caroline Bartlett Crane to Mrs. Robert M. LaFollette, 14 January 1911, Crane Papers.

33Crane, "History of Meat Inspection."

34Paul Kellogg to Caroline Bartlett Crane, 1 November 1909, Crane Papers.

35Albert Shaw to Norman Hapgood of *Colliers,* 18 March 1912; and Albert Shaw to George Lorimor of *Saturday Evening Post*, 19 March 1985, Crane Papers.

36Filler, *Crusaders of American Liberalism*, pp. 360–70. (In a chapter titled "The End of Muckraking" Filler indicates that after 1910 magazines showed less and less enthusiasm for the investigative article or series.)

37Cameron MacKenzie to Albert Shaw, 17 April 1912, Crane Papers.

38U. S. House of Representatives, *Proceedings of Hearings before the Committee on Expenditures in the Department of Agriculture on Nelson Resolution 51* (Washington: Government Printing Office, 1912), p. 8. (Hereafter, references to the hearings will be entitled *Nelson Proceedings.*)

39Caroline Bartlett Crane to Augustus Warren Crane, 2 May 1912; and "Mrs. Crane Compliments Mayor, Council," *Fort Dodge Messenger* (6 May 1912).

40Augustus Warren Crane to Caroline Bartlett Crane, 22 April 1912, Crane Papers.

41*Nelson Proceedings*, p. 4.

42*Nelson Proceedings*, p. 4.

43"Oppose Meat Inquiry," *New York Times* (2 May 1912).

44*Nelson Proceedings,* pp. 151–52; and Caroline Bartlett Crane to Augustus Warren Crane, 8 May 1912, Crane Papers.

45*Nelson Proceedings*, pp. 151–52; Caroline Bartlett Crane to Augustus Warren Crane, 2 February 1912, Crane Papers; and Charles N. Glaab and A. Theodore Brown, *A History of Urban America* (New York: The MacMillan Company, 1967), p. 196. According to Glaab and Brown, John M. Patterson, the president of NCR, was a tireless advocate of municipal reform.

[46]Harvey W. Wiley, "The Attack on Caroline Bartlett Crane," *Good House-keeping* 55 (July 1912), pp. 107–08.

[47]"U. S. Inspected and Passed," *La Follette's* 4 (12 June 1912), 14.

[48]Caroline Bartlett Crane to Augustus Warren Crane, 10 May 1912, Crane Papers. A. D. Melvin was chief of the Bureau of Animal Industry; John R. Mohler, chief of the pathological division; and S. E. Bennett, the chief inspector in Chicago.

[49]*Nelson Proceedings*, pp. 56–57.

[50]*Nelson Proceedings*, pp. 96–98.

[51]R. Van Orman, "Municipal Meat Inspection and Municipal Slaughter Houses," *The American City* 11 (July 1914), 14.

[52]*Nelson Proceedings*, pp. 115–19.

[53]After she was denied access to the documents Congressman Nelson found 1907 and 1908 *Service Announcements* in the Division of Documents of the Congressional Library.

[54]*Nelson Proceedings*, pp. 130–32, 137–38.

[55]*Nelson Proceedings*, pp. 115–19.

[56]"Meat Inspection Fair," *New York Sun* (10 May 1912).

[57]"Wiley Upholds Woman in Beef Test Charges," *New York Sun* (10 May 1912).

[58]*Nelson Proceedings*, pp. 128–40.

[59]*Nelson Proceedings*, pp. 112–13.

[60]*Nelson Proceedings*, p. 108.

[61]*Nelson Proceedings*, p. 109.

[62]John Nelson to Caroline Bartlett Crane, 15 April 1912; and Caroline Bartlett Crane to Augustus Warren Crane, 16 May 1912, Crane Papers.

[63]Caroline Bartlett Crane to Augustus Warren Crane, 17 May 1912, Crane Papers.

[64]John Nelson to Mrs. S. S. Crockett, 21 March 1914, Crane Papers.

[65]Caroline Bartlett Crane to Augustus Warren Crane, 27 May 1912, Crane Papers.

[66]Caroline Bartlett Crane to Augustus Warren Crane, 21 May 1912, Crane Papers.

[67]"Oppose Meat Inquiry," *New York Times* (2 May 1912); "Bad Meat Inquiry Today," *New York Times* (8 May 1912); "Victims of Bad Meat," *New York Times* (12 May 1912); "Saw Bad Beef Used in Making Sausages," *New York Times* (14 May 1912); "Exposes Packing Methods," *New York Times* (16 May 1912); and "Meat Inquiry Deferred," *New York Times* (17 May 1912).

[68]Charles Edward Russell, "Seasoning Our Diet of Garbage," *The Coming Nation* (15 June 1912), 7, 14, 16.

[69]U. S. House of Representatives, *Proceedings of Hearing Before the Committee on Rules, House of Representatives Under House Resolution 545 Concerning Department Press Agents*, 21 May 1912 (Washington: Government Printing Office, 1912); and "U. S. Inspected and Passed," *LaFollette's* 4 (12 June 1912), 14.

[70]U. S. House of Representatives, *Proceedings of Hearing Before the Committee on Rules, House of Representatives Under House Resolution 545 Concerning Department Press Agents*, p. 19.

[71]Fox, "History of the Equal Suffrage Movement in Michigan," p. 101.

[72]Anna Howard Shaw to Caroline Bartlett Crane, 14 September 1912, Crane Papers.

[73]Fox, "History of the Equal Suffrage Movement in Michigan," p. 101.

[74]Fox, "History of the Equal Suffrage Movement in Michigan," p. 101.

[75]Bennett, "Cleaning Up the American City," *American Magazine*, p. 44–48.

[76]Harper, *The History of Suffrage*, 5: 333; and Caroline Bartlett Crane to Augustus Warren Crane, 22 November 1912, Crane Papers.

[77]Caroline Bartlett Crane to Augustus Warren Crane, 4 March 1913, Crane Papers; "Rev. Caroline Bartlett Crane to March with Suffragists in Washington, D. C.," *Kalamazoo Gazette* (3 March 1913).

[78]Caroline Bartlett Crane, "U. S. Inspected and Passed," *Pearson's Magazine*, 3 (March 1913), pp. 258–68, and following articles in April, May, June, and July.

[79]Filler, *Crusaders for American Liberalism*, pp. 370–71.

[80]Samuel Hopkins Adams, "U. S. Inspected and Passed: A Review of Caroline Bartlett Crane's Striking Series of Articles on Bad Meat and Worse Politics in *Pearson's Magazine*," *The Survey*, 6 (September 1913), pp. 695–99; and reprinted in the *General Federation Magazine* 12 (January 1914), pp. 15–16.

[81]Ibid.

[82]Adams, "U. S. Inspected and Passed: A Review," 698.

[83]Belle C. LaFollette, "A Political and Hygienic Outrage; Are the Packers to Gain A Control Over Our Great Food Staples Too Strong for the American People Ever to Break" *LaFollette's* 5 (16 August 1913), pp. 5, 12; Caroline Bartlett Crane, "Municipal Abattoirs: The Hope of the American Consumer for Clean and Healthy Meat," *LaFollette's* 5 (15 August 1913), pp. 12–14 (reprint from *Pearson's*).

[84]"Meat Inspection Declared a Farce," *Philadelphia Record* (2 March 1913); and "Clean Meat for Philadelphia," *City Club Bulletin* 6 (28 March 1913), 363–72.

[85]U. S. Department of Agriculture, "The History of Inspection Programs and the Debate on Current Procedures," excerpted from the National Academy of Sciences, Meat and Poultry Inspection—the Scientific Basis of the Nation's Program, July 1985, and U. S. Department of Agriculture, Food Safety and Quality Service, Federal Meat & Poultry Inspection Program, "Inspection Milestones: A Brief History of Meat and Poultry Inspection in the United States"(1985).

[86]Interview with Clarence Pals, Director of the USDA meat inspection service from 1960 to 1965, 7 September 1985.

[87]Caroline Bartlett Crane, "Report of Caroline Bartlett Crane," *Washington State Board of Health Quarterly Bulletin* 4 (January–February–March 1913), p. 1.

MOTHERHOOD AND WAR

In 1914 two events diverted Crane from her efforts at reform: she and Warren decided to adopt children; and war broke out in Europe. In January 1914 Crane went to Boston to talk with the principal of the Maine Industrial School for Girls, who had located a male child for adoption.[1] In February she made another trip East and brought home an infant son, whom they named Warren Bartlett.

Despite being fifty-five years old, Crane was as enthusiastic about the child as any young mother. She kept a diary of her first six months of motherhood, reporting almost every utterance and diaper change.[2] About a year after Bartlett's adoption the Cranes' adopted Juliana, who was in a Michigan orphanage. She thought it was a great idea to make them twins, so she listed their birthdays as 25 May 1913.[3] She spent much of her time during the next two years with her babies, but did find energy to conduct a sanitary survey in Uniontown, Pennsylvania, in 1914.[4] She refused an invitation from the Red Cross to use her municipal sanitation skills to help reconstruct Belgian cities destroyed in early action of the war in Europe.[5]

Experiences at the Brown Thrush continued to be among Caroline's and Warren's most treasured private moments. Warren took the children to the cottage for the first time when they were about one year old. It was mid-summer, and Warren carried Bartlett down to the lake and watched him crawl fearlessly toward the water's edge. Gurgling with delight, the infant crept into the water until it reached his little mouth. He laughed and spanked the surface with his flattened hands. Both children learned to swim at an early age, and it was a great event for them to come to the cottage with their parents.[6]

Bartlett, Caroline said, tried to take his first steps at the cottage during his second summer with the Cranes:

> He had taken a faltering step or two from chair to chair but one day he surprised and thrilled me by climbing up by the sofa near the inner door and walking with many erratic but determined steps straight across the porch to the outside door, a distance of some twelve feet, where he succumbed with such a delightful crow of conquest that I rushed to pick him up and properly kiss him.[7]

Caroline said that for some reason cows were Bartlett's special interest and delight as a child. As Caroline and Warren were driving along the road, Bartlett would say "cow" when one of the animals appeared even upon the most distant horizon. When the children were small the Cranes had a pet dog, Barney. Caroline said that it did not take Barney long to achieve the position of Bartlett's guardian and caretaker. "I would wheel him to the Post Office, and leave him in Barney's care for the few moments I went inside," Caroline added. "He always stood watchful and erect as if he felt his responsibility and took great pride therein."[8]

The addition of the children enhanced Caroline's and Warren's relationship. They called each other "Mama" and "Papa" in their letters. Caroline also called the children "Piggie Wiggie" and "Piggie Woggle," apparently in connection with one of her favorite private names for Warren, "Piggy."[9]

On two occasions in 1915, Caroline turned down oppor-
tunities to assume a leadership role in the Women's Peace Party, a
group organized to protest U. S. involvement in the war. In
February she rejected an invitation from Jane Addams, president
of the party, to be a delegate to the Women's Peace Congress.[10]
The Congress had been conceived by Dr. Aletta Jacobs of
Holland, a leader in the Women's International Suffrage Alliance.
Addams led a delegation of fifty members of the Women's Peace
Party to the Congress in April.[11] Again in December, Crane
refused invitations from Jane Addams and Henry Ford, who asked
her to join them on the Ford Peace Ship.[12] The auto manufacturer
had leased the Scandinavian-American steamship Oscar II to take
Americans first to Norway and Sweden, where they would be
joined by other peace advocates, and then to The Hague, where
delegates would conduct an International Conference of Neutral
Nations.

By the time the ship left New York the public considered
the project a grand folly.[13] The idea of the peace expedition and
conference of neutral nations originated in the Women's Peace
Party, but Ford had more than enthusiastically embraced the idea.
Crane was critical of the hurry with which the trip was put
together. The complex mission was organized in only ten days,
with the ship passing through the war zone to get to Holland. One
hundred Americans were to make the voyage, but many
prominent peace advocates rejected the invitations. The prestige of
the mission suffered greatly when at the last minute Addams did
not make the trip because of illness, and Ford abandoned the
cruise and returned to America when the ship arrived in Europe.[14]

"It is my own belief that Mr. Ford, with the very best of
intentions, took the peace movement largely out of the hands of
Miss Addams," Crane said in a newspaper column explaining her

decision to stay home.[15] She had been supportive of Addams's efforts to induce President Wilson to take part in a conference of neutral nations, and Crane had worked for such a conference by making speeches and collecting signatures on petitions. She believed, however, that Ford's action was "a little meddlesome." In commenting on her decision not to participate in the Ford peace mission, Crane advocated support of the Preparedness Movement. She said:

> But I also believe in the imminent duty of this country to prepare to maintain its own peace, dignity and honor by increasing and strengthening its military and naval defenses now. And I also believe that no private individual or corporation should make money by this business, thus having a direct financial interest in wars and war scares and casting a certain blight of suspicion over party and congressional leaders and prominent persons generally who advocate a policy of military preparedness.[16]

Crane's views contrasted sharply with those held by many women's movement leaders. Jane Addams and Florence Kelley, director of the Consumers' League, were pacifists, and several women's organizations had peace divisions that favored pacifism.[17]

During this year John Nolen, city planning expert from Cambridge, Massachusetts, had been instrumental in making arrangements for Crane to make a sanitary and sociologic survey of several cities in Ireland. Nolen had arranged the trip with the Lord Lieutenant of Ireland and Lady Aberdeen. All the preliminaries were completed, but the trip was postponed because Ireland was in the throes of the debate over Home Rule and the Ulster question.[18]

Crane did make one survey in 1916, her final one, in Kankakee, Illinois.[19] Between 1908 and 1916 she had conducted surveys in sixty-two cities in fourteen states, including three statewide surveys. She had received praise and faced adversity, but she always had faith that some measure of reform would come from her crusades for civic righteousness.[20]

When America entered the war on the side of the allies in 1917, yet another career opened for Caroline Bartlett Crane. A great outpouring of patriotic idealism followed America's entry, and many women's organizations joined in the patriotic fervor over the "war to end war," the war that would make "the world safe for democracy." To corral some of this enthusiasm generated by the war effort, the Council of National Defense, composed of the Secretaries of War, the Navy, the Interior, Agriculture, Commerce, and Labor, created the Woman's Committee. On 21 April 1917 ten women were appointed to the council by its chairperson, Anna Howard Shaw, former suffrage leader.[21] Shaw appointed Crane president of the Michigan Women's Committee of National Defense.

The purpose of the committee was to

> coordinate the activities and the resources of the organized and unorganized women of the country that their power may be immediately utilized in time of need, and to supply a new and direct channel of communication and cooperation between women and governmental departments.[22]

After receiving her appointment as head of the Michigan division Crane issued a call for a statewide meeting in Kalamazoo, and twenty-two women's organizations responded. As a result of the meeting, a state headquarters was established in Kalamazoo.[23] In its early months the committee was concerned mainly with establishing itself in counties, cities, and townships throughout

Michigan. Every county except one was organized.[24] In July,
Governor Albert Sleeper appointed a Women's Committee on War
Preparedness to coordinate activities among the Woman's
Committee, the Council of National Defense, and the State War
Preparedness Board. Crane was named chairman of the commit-
tee.[25]

   That Fall Crane went to Washington for a Women's
Defense Committee meeting. It was the first time that she had been
there since the adoption of her children. She recalled her last trip
to the city, when she had testified before a congressional
committee regarding her findings on meat inspection, in a letter to
Warren: "I cannot but feel, dear, that I am a much better woman
than when I was under this roof [the Hotel Driscoll] last." She
said that she looked at the pictures of Bartlett and Juliana and
recalled when they did not have children: "I was just beginning to
feel the lack of them painfully. And now we have had them so
long that it is hard to realize we were without children four-fifths
of our life together." Crane wrote that she thought the United
States had to fight the war "for all the children."[26]

   Under Crane's leadership the Michigan division became
involved in several projects, the most successful of which were
voluntary wartime registration of women for service, food
production, and food conservation efforts. On the national level,
the registration of American women over sixteen years of age was
the most formidable project undertaken. Authorized by the
Federal government, the registration was recorded on cards
approved by the Census Bureau. It took three months, but a total
of 900,000 Michigan women were registered, the greatest number
in any state.[27] The women were asked to list occupations; 75%
listed housewife. The registration cards were used by a placement
office to put women in contact with any organization—not just the

Red Cross and war-related agencies—that needed volunteers, including hospitals, poorhouses, infant clinics, settlement houses, charity agencies, schools, health offices, and city and county agencies. One of the most striking demonstrations of the value of the registration came after the signing of the Armistice in 1918. When the nation was hit by the Spanish influenza epidemic, women who had registered as nurses and nurses' aides were quickly located through the Women's Committee files.

The first of the Michigan division's departments to organize was that devoted to food production. In fact, this work was started two months before the National Defense Council's Women's Committee was organized. On March 27 a meeting of the heads of Michigan's women's organizations was called in Lansing by Nellie Clark of Kalamazoo, then president of the Michigan State Suffrage Association, acting under instructions of the NAWSA. As a result of the meeting an organization called "The Michigan Women's Committee for Patriotic Service" was formed, and Crane was elected state chairman.[28]

Increased food production was the work that seemed at the time to require emergency action. After consultation with the extension department of the Michigan Agricultural College (later to become Michigan State University), a campaign was started to induce rural women to undertake seed corn testing and to disinfect oats for smut so that the acreage of these crops could be increased. These efforts would relieve men for the heavier tasks of plowing and planting. Seed potatoes at that time also were scarce, so the Women's Committee circulated coupon pledges against eating potatoes.[29] The pledges failed to produce enough tubers to meet the great demand, but two thousand bushels were purchased in northern Michigan and elsewhere and sold at cost in Kalamazoo and neighboring counties to persons pledged to plant and faithfully cultivate them. Great emphasis was placed on the necessity of each family raising sufficient food to be stored, canned, dried, or otherwise preserved. To encourage amateur gardeners, especially children, a special "I Am Pledged" button was designed, and more than 100,000 were sold for a dime or given away.[30] City vegetable markets were established in Kalamazoo, Grand Rapids, Lansing, Marshall, and elsewhere.

Food conservation was another important project for the Woman's Committee. The Michigan committee printed and distributed 250,000 Hoover Pledge Cards in the summer of 1917.[31] Women taking the pledge promised to plan meals carefully and to conserve food when possible. In June, 1918, in Detroit, Crane spoke before the National Municipal League on "The Housewife and the Marketing Problem." Copies of the address were sent to the units of the Woman's Committee in the hope that the plan would prevent waste of food grown in response to the appeal for increased production.[32] In several speeches Crane warned against reduced home food consumption that would be harmful to children's nutrition.[33]

On April 6, 1918, the first anniversary of America's entry into the war, the Children's Bureau of the Labor Department and the National Woman's Committee, with the approval of President Wilson, jointly launched a campaign for American children called the "Children's Year."[34] One impetus for the campaign was the appalling number of men rejected from conscription because of health problems, many of which could be traced to neglect in infancy and childhood. Child welfare thus became a national policy concern, and the infant mortality rate became a health issue. The Children's Bureau urged increased public protection of the health and general welfare of infants and children and of mothers before and after the birth of children; relief for mothers of young children from the necessity of working away from home; a campaign to keep children from leaving school prematurely and to get back into school the large number of children who had been lured away by war demands and war wages; more and better public recreation facilities for children and adolescents; and better public care and oversight of individuals who were generally dependent, deficient, and neglected.[35]

Crane immediately organized the Michigan "Children's Year" committee. The most ambitious undertaking of the Michigan Child Welfare Committee was the "Children's Year Special."[36] Crane convinced several railroad companies to donate cars and engines for a statewide "Children's Year Special" train. Originally, the train was slated to travel for six weeks, from October 1 to November 16, 1918, and to stop in sixty-five cities and villages; but when the Spanish Influenza epidemic began to assume serious proportions, the train was called in. When health conditions improved the Children's Year Special resumed its journey,[37] though the number of its stops was reduced to fifty-five.

The exterior of the train was gaily decorated with banners and posters that announced "Uncle Sam Wants You to Visit This Car," and "Bring Your Babies and Children to be Weighed and Measured." The train featured cars decorated as attractive exhibits, and literature for both children and parents urged safety and provided information on mother and child care. Another section of the train was devoted to an examination dressing room for the children, and an examination room where children were weighed and measured by physicians and nurses. The train drew big crowds in several counties and uncovered many health problems among its visitors.

18.

"The Children's Year Special" was a special project organized by the Michigan Woman's Committee during World War I. Nurses and physicians examined children brought to the train.

Crane and the committee also were involved in "back to school" and "stay in school" campaigns in Michigan, and the Child Welfare Committee was instrumental in securing first-time funding of vocational and physical education programs.[38] During the war Crane held the position of special agent for Michigan for the U. S. Department of Labor's Children's Bureau, and following the armistice she received special recognition for her service in the form of a bronze medal from the agency.

The Woman's Committee worked with several national and state government and relief organizations and vigorously supported the League to Enforce Peace, an organization founded in 1915 that advocated the creation of an international league of nations to keep the peace and prevent war. The League to Enforce Peace appointed Crane a member of the National Executive Committee with the special duty of advancing the League of Nations movement among the women's organizations of Michigan.[39]

When news came of the armistice in November, 1918, the Woman's Committee was at the height of its activity. Crane believed that her organization could be as useful in peacetime as it had been during the war. In fact, she thought that most of its activities should become permanent in every community. The war, she said, had revealed "to us how much of our common everyday duty to society was being neglected."[40] She was dismayed when Governor Sleeper urged all state war organizations to disband. She protested the governor's action, and Sleeper reconsidered, ordering all wartime organizations to continue functioning.[41]

Sleeper later appointed Crane as a delegate to the Win the War for Permanent Peace Conference in Philadelphia in May, 1918, and named her as one of seven members of the state's Reconstruction Committee.[42] The National Municipal League also appointed Crane to serve as a member of the Forty on Reconstruction and War Problems.[43] A year later, on May 22, 1919, the Michigan Woman's Committee was finally dissolved and its property given to a newly-formed State Community Council Commission, which had been created by the legislature on the recommendation of the state's Reconstruction Committee.[44]

For her work with the Michigan Woman's Committee, Crane received no salary, and financial records show that she spent $1,000 of her own money in its work.[45] Crane and the thousands of women—by their service to the Council of National Defense Women's Committee—served their country, and by doing so, did much to advance the struggle for woman suffrage.

NOTES

[1]Caroline Bartlett Crane to Augustus Warren Crane, 31 January 1914, Crane Papers.

[2]Caroline Bartlett Crane, "Baby," a handwritten manuscript ca. 1914, Crane Papers.

[3]Interview with Juliana Crane, 6 December 1983.

[4]Caroline Bartlett Crane, *A Sanitary Survey of Uniontown, Pennsylvania* (Uniontown: Women's Civic League, 1914).

[5]"Mrs. Crane Refuses to Go on Ford Peace Ship," *Kalamazoo Telegraph-Press* (30 November 1915).

[6]Crane, "The Brown Thrush," in Recollections, p. 1.

[7]Crane, "The Brown Thrush," p. 2.

[8]Crane, "The Brown Thrush," p. 3.

[9]Caroline Bartlett Crane to Augustus Warren Crane, 9 September 1914, Crane Papers; Caroline Bartlett Crane to Augustus Warren Crane, 23 September 1914, Crane Papers.

[10]"Mrs. Crane Refuses," *Kalamazoo Telegraph-Press* (30 November 1915).

[11]Allen F. Davis, *American Heroine: The Life and Legend of Jane Addams* (New York: Oxford University Press, 1973), pp. 237–40.

[12]Henry Ford to Caroline Bartlett Crane, 28 November 1915, Crane Papers; Jane Addams to Caroline Bartlett Crane, 24 November 1915, Crane Papers; and Henry Ford to Caroline Bartlett Crane, 27 November 1915, Crane Papers.

[13]Davis, *American Heroine: The Life and Legend of Jane Addams*, pp. 237–38.

[14]Davis, *American Heroine*, pp. 237–38.

[15]Caroline Bartlett Crane, "The Ford Peace Expedition," ca. 1915 newspaper clipping, *Kalamazoo Progressive Herald*, Crane Papers.

[16]Crane, "Ford Peace Expedition," ca. 1915 newspaper clipping, *Kalamazoo Progressive Herald*, Crane Papers.

[17]J. Stanley Lemons, *The Woman Citizen: Social Feminism in the 1920s* (Urbana: University of Illinois Press, 1973), p. 4.

[18]Caroline Bartlett Crane to John Nolen in care of Vice Regal Lodge, Dublin, Ireland, 23 February 1914, Crane Papers; Caroline Bartlett Crane to John Nolen, 15 May 1914, Crane Papers.

[19]"Sanitary Expert Offers Suggestions for Improvement of Local Conditions," *Kankakee Daily Republican* (20 October 1916).

[20]*Notable American Women 1907–1950: A Biographical Dictionary*, vol. 1, s. v., "Caroline Bartlett Crane," pp. 401–02.

21Women's Committee of the United States Council of National Defense, *The Woman's Committee of the United States Council of National Defense: An Interpretative Report*, by Emily Newell Blair (Washington: Government Printing Office, 1920), pp. 9–15; and Lemons, *The Woman Citizen*, pp. 16–18.

22Caroline Bartlett Crane, *History of the Work of the Women's Committee (Michigan Division) Council of National Defense During the World War* (Lansing, Michigan: State Administrative Office, 1922), p. 6. (Hereafter, the booklet will be referred to as *History of the Michigan Committee*.)

23Crane, *History of the Michigan Committee*, p. 6.

24Crane, *History of the Michigan Committee*, p. 8.

25Crane, *History of the Michigan Committee*, p. 9.

26Caroline Bartlett Crane to Augustus Warren Crane, 24 October 1917, Crane Papers.

27Crane, *History of the Michigan Committee*, p. 22.

28Crane, *History of the Michigan Committee*, p. 32.

29Crane, *History of the Michigan Committee*, p. 33.

30Crane, *History of the Michigan Committee*, p. 34; and "I Am Pledged," *Kalamazoo Gazette* (12 July 1917).

31Crane, *History of the Michigan Committee*, p. 36. Herbert Hoover was Secretary of Commerce and in charge of all food conservation projects.

32Caroline Bartlett Crane, "The Housewife and the Marketing Problem," speech given to the National Municipal League, Detroit, 11 July 1918, reprinted in Crane Papers; and Crane, *History of the Michigan Committee*, p. 36.

33"Don't Curtail Food Supply for Children," *Flint* (Michigan) *Journal* (12 July 1917); "Grow Food, Aid Babes in War," *Detroit Free Press* (30 April 1917); and "Don't Let War Nip Children's Dinner," *Detroit Free Press* (12 August 1917).

[34]Crane, *History of the Michigan Committee*, p. 42; and Lemons, *The Woman Citizen*, p. 16.

[35]Crane, *History of the Michigan Committee*, p. 42.

[36]Crane, *History of the Michigan Committee*, p. 43; Ina J. N. Perkins, "Michigan Children's Year Special," *Public Health* 7 (April 1919), pp. 161–63 (published by Michigan State Board of Health).

[37]Crane, *History of the Michigan Committee*, pp. 44–45; and "Over 1,000 Babes are Measured in 1st Three Days," *Jackson* (Michigan) *Telegraph* (16 September 1918).

[38]Crane, *History of the Michigan Committee*, pp. 48–50, 52.

[39]Crane, *History of the Michigan Committee*, p. 68.

[40]Crane, *History of the Michigan Committee*, pp. 71–72.

[41]"Carry On is Slogan," *Carry On,* 23 November 1918, Crane Papers; "Women of State Will Not Relax," unidentified newspaper, n.d.; and Caroline Bartlett Crane to Franklin K. Lane (Chairman Field Division) of the Council of National Defense, 14 November 1918, Crane Papers.

[42]Commission certificate, Crane Papers.

[43]Crane, *History of the Michigan Committee*, p. 72; and Reconstruction Committee to Governor Albert E. Sleeper, *Reconstruction in Michigan*, 11 March 1919, Crane Papers.

[44]Crane, *History of the Michigan Committee*, p. 73.

[45]Financial ledger of Michigan Committee, Crane Papers.

A CITIZEN

After the Armistice, Crane confined most of her activism to housing reform and to the work of the League of Women Voters. Although many women's leaders feared the war would disrupt the advancement of suffrage, women's organizations eagerly became involved in war mobilization work, and the NAWSA publicized the roles played by Anna Howard Shaw and other suffragists in the Woman's Committee for National Defense.[1]

By 1918 woman suffrage had gained many new supporters in Michigan. For example, in 1913 a suffrage referendum lost by 100,000 votes, but in 1918 a similar suffrage referendum won by 25,000 supporters. In June of 1919 the Sixty-Sixth Congress approved the Nineteenth Amendment, and by the spring of 1920 the required two-thirds of the states had ratified it. Instead of harming the suffrage movement, the war turned out to be boon: women had done their part for the battle overseas, and suffrage at home was their reward.[2]

In a speech before the Detroit Federation of Women's Clubs, Crane urged women to be "humble and cautious" in their use of the vote. Women, she said, should forget their criticisms of men and the society men created:

> Always the criticism of thoughtful women has been that the state has been fathered and not mothered. We do not want to run things—all we want to do is to add the woman's point of

view and woman's experience to man's, and to stand shoulder
to shoulder with them to achieve a better order of things for
all of us.[3]

Crane was sixty-two years old in the Fall of 1920 and had
served her city, state, and country for more than three decades
before she voted for the first time in a national election.
Unfortunately, Anna Howard Shaw had not lived to see the
ratification of the Woman's Suffrage Amendment. In 1919 while
on a speaking tour with former President William Howard Taft to
promote the activities of the League to Enforce Peace, Shaw
became ill. On July 2 Lucy Anthony, a niece of Susan B.
Anthony, wired Crane of Shaw's death and urged her to come at
once to Shaw's home in suburban Philadelphia. There Crane
presided at funeral services held in Shaw's home, reading the
Twenty-Third Psalm and other short Bible chapters. Suffrage
leader Carrie Lane Chapman Catt delivered the eulogy.[4]

On April 1, 1920, Warren's mother, Julia, who had resided
in Caroline and Warren's home since 1897, died.[5] Shortly after
her death the Cranes purchased a home at 1425 Hillcrest Avenue
and converted the 406 Rose Street house into an office for
Warren. They also sold the Brown Thrush property, which had
been their retreat since their marriage, and purchased property at
Sharon on the Little Manistee River.[6]

Crane's letters to her husband reveal no great emotional
crisis during this period, but she was still prone to nervous and
depressed states. In 1918 she mentioned her "horrible fits of
depression."[7] Crane worried a great deal about her children. Her
daughter had difficulty in school, and she believed that Bartlett,
who was rather bright, was rather lazy. The letters reveal that Crane
expected her children to meet her own high academic and moral
standards.[8]

In 1922 Warren went to England and then to Germany with two pioneer radiologists. In Frankfort the physicians each purchased a deep radiation therapy machine; Warren identified these as the first three used in North America. One of the physicians was a professor at the University of Michigan Medical College; the other was associated with the x-ray department at the University of Toronto.[9] While Warren was in Germany his wife wrote complaining that Bartlett had "lazy habits." She added, "Bartlett puts everything off—never does anything voluntarily."[10]

In spite of her exasperation over her son, the family's home life was happy. Just like younger mothers, Crane went to all the parent and teacher conferences and school meetings. Christmases were the happiest time of the year for the children. Each Christmas, Caroline's gift from Warren also had an original poem attached. Despite their busy schedules, the family made several trips: Juliana's favorite was to the Field Museum in Chicago.[11] During this time Crane's health was very good. In 1924, however, she broke her hip in a fall, and she continued to have problems with her left eye.[12]

In 1919 the NAWSA formed the National League of Women Voters (NLWV) to continue the women's rights movement after Federal suffrage had been attained.[13] Crane served as a director of the Michigan League of Women Voters for twelve years,[14] taught NLWV seminars on a wide variety of subjects,[15] and provided leadership for the league's department of International Cooperation to Prevent War. She also became involved in the American Peace Association,[16] which was not a pacifist organization but a conservative group interested in disarmament and outlawing war. In addition, Crane continued her

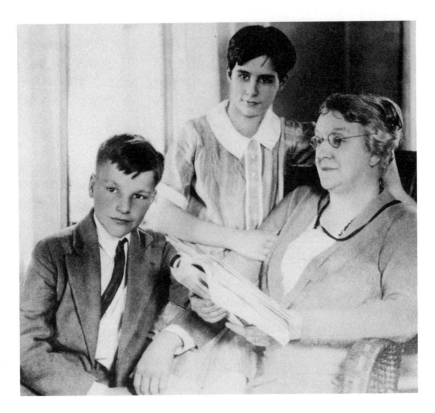

19.

Caroline and her adopted children; Bartlett, left, and Juliana, right (from a scrapbook in the collection of Crane's grandaughter, Julie Durham).

20.

Dr. A. W. Crane with children (from a scrapbook in the collection of Crane's grandaughter, Julie Durham).

involvement in the League to Enforce Peace, serving as a director of the Michigan branch.[17]

During the winter of 1923–24, Carrie Lane Chapman Catt, former NAWSA president, emerged as a major leader in the woman's peace movement, establishing the National Committee for the Cause and Cure of War. The organization was a clearing-house for the peace interests of nine of the largest women's organizations[18] and supported world-wide disarmament proposals and the World Court. In 1924, 463 delegates from such organiza-tions as the Women's Christian Temperance Union, the General Federation of Women's Clubs, and the League of Women Voters gathered in Washington for the first of fourteen annual National Conferences on the Cause and Cure of War. Crane, representing the Michigan League of Women Voters, was a delegate to seven of the first ten conferences.[19]

At the formation of the NLWV two philosophies vied for control of its future. Catt wanted the organization to be political, while Jane Addams believed that it should be the conduit for the organizing of women's municipal housekeeping work at the community level. At NLWV's convention in 1920 a compromise was reached. The league's mission would be "education for citizenship, reforming the electorate, and promoting a more just society."[20]

Above all other interests, the chief thrust of Crane's civic activism during the last decades of her life was housing reform. On November 12, 1919, she testified as the first witness in a hearing before a Congressional committee, urging passage of a bill to create an office of housing and living conditions in the Department of Labor.[21] The bill was unsuccessful, but the hearing helped popularize the family housing cause. Crane told the Committee on Public Buildings and Grounds that there were housing shortages even in small cities such as Alma, where business slums were used for living quarters. She testified that in Michigan a "terrific housing shortage" was crippling industry as well. "In my home town of Kalamazoo there are many industries which are practically at a standstill, and which will have to move away from us because we can not house the people," she said. "In order to meet that situation we are making a great effort to raise funds, and have secured an option on 627 building sites, if we can raise the money to do the building."[22] Crane was convinced that providing family housing would improve the quality of life, especially for the children in America. "Unless you live in a decent home you can not bring up children as they should be brought up," she said.

In 1924, Crane wrote a series of articles on municipal sanitation for the *Woman Citizen*, the title taken by NAWSA's *Woman's Journal* after the enactment of suffrage. The publication was the official organ of the NLWV[23] until 1921, when it severed official ties with the NLWV, although it continued to provide space for the league to print its news and notices. In an effort to reach a wider audience, the magazine in 1928 again called itself *Woman's Journal.*

Several of Crane's articles revived her earlier urban health reform themes: street sanitation, smoke abatement, and garbage disposal.[24] In 1925 she became a member of the magazine's staff of contributing editors,[25] and at the same time she found fresher issues. In articles published in *Woman Citizen* she warned of the danger of slums in small towns and in rural areas. Michigan had a housing code that excluded from jurisdiction towns with a population fewer than ten thousand people. Crane said that it was absurd to exclude small towns from jurisdiction and cited several examples to illustrate that, left to their own devices, small towns will have housing problems as severe as those in large cities.[26] In an article entitled the "Suburbs Beyond the Law" she argued that suburban developments beyond the city limits should not be excluded from the jurisdiction of state and local housing and sanitation laws, as they were in Michigan and many other states. Possessed of a great deal of foresight, she understood the problems that would accompany future urban developments.[27] Crane was critical of county and township governments' lack of incentive for mandating housing codes and inspection laws because most of the people who bought the new suburban homes were from the cities. "County organization is generally denounced as the 'jungle of American politics,' an anachronism which threatens to become our great national pest, as cities everywhere spill over into the surrounding rural territory," she wrote.[28] Crane said that the best protection for the home buyer in the suburbs was a self-policing housing industry and honest real estate developers and agents.

Reviving the issues of milk and meat hygiene, Crane wrote two articles on what she called the "new kitchen-mindedness." She urged housewives to purchase only pasteurized milk and bemoaned the continued lack of municipal meat inspection. She quoted USDA figures that contended that six billion pounds of meat consumed annually were still exempt from state or federal meat inspection.[29] Other articles in *Woman Citizen* and *Woman's Journal* carrying Crane's byline focused on jury service for women, women in the pulpit, and the problems caused by the relentless cutting of Michigan's timber.[30]

The high point for Crane in the 1920s, however, was her success in the national "Better Homes in America" movement to encourage the development of new housing trends and architecture. The idea for "Better Homes" originated with Mrs. William Brown Meloney, editor of the *Delineator* magazine.[31] Herbert Hoover, then Secretary of Commerce, served as president of the organization, and members of its advisory committee included President Calvin Coolidge, several cabinet members, and other important industrial and civic leaders.[32] In 1923 and 1924 the Better Homes Committee asked community leaders to construct family homes based on innovative designs and to submit the plans and details of their projects to be judged in national contests each year.

During the winter of 1924, Crane received a letter from Hoover urging her to organize a project in Kalamazoo. At the age of sixty-five, she accepted the challenge and threw all her energies into the contest.[33] On March 3 she held a meeting of interested citizens and immediately obtained their support. The Kalamazoo Realtors' Association provided the site; a contractor volunteered the labor; an architect offered to turn the committee's (Crane's) plans into drawings that the contractor could use; several building firms contributed construction materials; and other businesses supplied the decorator, the landscape architect, furniture, and equipment.[34]

As in her 1904 Kalamazoo cleanup project, Crane's crusade involved local children who brought topsoil in wagons to the site and planted a vegetable garden.[35] The city's garden clubs offered to help with landscaping. It was to be the house that everyone built, and Crane managed to whip up to fever pitch Kalamazoo's sense of community pride. The small house went up almost as fast as an Amish barn: the cornerstone was put in place only eleven days after the ground-breaking. In less than seven weeks the contractors turned over the keys to the local Better Homes committee.[36]

On June 25 Crane received a letter from Herbert Hoover notifying her that the Kalamazoo structure had won first place from among 1,500 entries. "Your demonstration was helpful to

21.

"Everyman's House" in Kalamazoo was the winner of the 1924 Better Homes design project.

every type of family, whether it rents or owns its home, through its selection of equipment, furnishing, decoration, and its kitchen contest," Hoover said.[37] Furthermore, he complimented the committee on designing a house that would be within the financial reach of many Americans.

Crane called the home "Everyman's House," emphasizing her desire to design a home that families could afford. The committee had resolved early in the planning stages to construct a house for a "family in which the father has a hard time making both ends meet and the mother does all the work in the house."[38] The committee believed it had met that goal when it tallied up its bills. The white frame colonial house would cost the average family from $5,000 to $7,000. It had cost the committee $5,400.[39]

The *Delineator* called the design a "new type of architecture," and the magazine said that Kalamazoo's entry won because its design was based on the needs of a mother and her infant. The city celebrated its victory with a Better Homes Week and a showing of the "revolutionary house." The mayor was the first to pass up the walk, past the dwarf Christmas trees, to the front door. He was welcomed by four children and their mother, who offered him the key to the city. During the week, twenty thousand visitors saw the nationally honored house.[40]

Most of the houses built during that time were arranged so that the nursery was on the second floor. In planning their contest entry, the committee had replaced a first-floor dining room with a nursery. Also for the convenience of the mother, the bathroom was located on the first floor of the two-story house. The small but complete facility enabled the mother to bathe her infants or supervise the baths of the somewhat older children without climbing stairs.[41] Another novel idea was a window above the kitchen sink that provided the housewife with a view as she washed dishes.

Crane wrote in detail about the project in a book entitled *Everyman's House*, published by Doubleday, Page and Company in 1925. Although it received several reviews, mostly favorable, the book never sold well. Crane blamed the publisher, claiming the company did not attempt to boost sales with advertising and other promotions. Eventually, at a reduced price of thirty-five cents each, the Better Homes national committee purchased eight hundred of the 2,500 books printed. The volumes had originally sold for $2.00 each.[42] Crane made the purchase arrangement with the Better Homes committee to keep the books from what she thought of as the disgrace of the bargain tables.

The Better Homes demonstration project brought Crane renewed acclaim, especially as a housing expert. In 1928 the Michigan Housing Association was formed, and Crane was named first vice president.[43] The purpose of the organization was to develop a plan for providing homes at cost for self-supporting, low income families through the establishment of garden communities.

The 1920s saw Crane involved in other arenas as well. In 1927 she found time to organize the women's auxiliary of the Michigan State Medical Society, and for her involvement in public health projects she was named an associate member of the Kalamazoo Academy of Medicine, a regional medical society.[44]

That year Crane also took on the Ku Klux Klan, which had brazenly endorsed a ticket of candidates in the Kalamazoo City Commission election. While Crane called the Klan a "moral and political menace," what disturbed her most was that the Women's Christian Temperance Union, of which she had been a longtime member, had endorsed the same seven candidates. Crane urged citizens to vote against the Klan ticket if "we wish to make ourselves free from a presumptuous, tyrannical, anonymous, irresponsible, fanatical, and exceedingly dangerous clique rule in Kalamazoo."[45]

In the late 1920s Crane also became an active member of the Kalamazoo Business and Professional Women's Club and continued her participation in the affairs of the Daughters of the American Revolution. During the mid- and late-1920s several superpatriotic organizations—including the DAR—accused many feminists, progressives, and liberals of being communists.[46] This "Spider Web" conspiracy controversy resulted in the compilation of blacklists that predated McCarthyism. In May, 1928, two members of the Kalamazoo chapter of the DAR—a mother and her daughter—claimed that Crane had accepted money from the Garland Fund, money ultraconservatives thought was provided by the Russian government to fund subversive propaganda in America.[47] The Garland Fund supported various liberal activities, including the NAACP. In response, Crane said, in part: "I here and now state to you upon my honor as a woman and a citizen that I have never received, directly or indirectly, by check, cash, or otherwise, one cent from the Garland Fund or Foundation."[48] Crane received a statement from her accusers that they had made "no charges," and it was read at the June 13, 1928, meeting of the Kalamazoo DAR chapter.[49] The statement said, in part: "I am willing to concede . . . that anything she [Crane] represents to you on any matter covering her personal conduct is beyond reproach."

Crane's job as mother was similarly fraught with challenges. In 1928 she hired tutors to help Juliana with her schoolwork. "When she [Juliana] is a sweet girl, as she always is now nearly all the time, I am happier in her company than with anyone else in the world except you . . . ," she wrote her husband.[50]

In contrast, she was convinced that she had "no influence" with Bartlett.[51]

On November 30, 1928, Crane suffered great personal grief when her brother, Charles, died after a mastoid operation in Denver, Colorado.[52] At the time of his death he was director of contractual relations for the United States Shipbuilding Corporation in Bristol, Virginia. Her own health was failing as well. In 1931 she wrote:

> I want to be a good wife, but no one, not even my husband, realizes the heavy shadow over me which is like the dark spot in my left eye. Wherever I go it is there, as that dark spot is wherever I look.[53]

Even the experts at John Hopkins Hospital in Baltimore were unable to diagnose her eye problem.[54] Crane wrote about her "shadow nature" again in 1932 in letters to her husband from Europe. Juliana had accompanied her mother to a Conference on International Relations in Geneva. Caroline became very emotional when she learned her daughter drank alcoholic beverages. Although Juliana did not drink to extreme, the point at stake was the "Bartlett Code" of abstinence. Crane believed her offspring had turned against her and that she would spend her old age "without the comfort of a loyal daughter." Crane also worried that she was embarrassing to her daughter because she was aging and sometimes appeared unkempt.[55]

Though aging, Crane continued to adapt to the needs of the world around her. She was appointed to the Mayor's Committee on Unemployment in Kalamazoo,[56] which sought ways to create jobs for the many unemployed. She also attended the National Conference on Unemployment, called by philosopher John Dewey, in Philadelphia.[57]

Even in the last years of her life Crane continued her fight against tuberculosis as a consultant for the National Tuberculosis Association.[58] She also persisted in her dedication to civic reform as a member of the executive council of the National Municipal League and as a member of the board of directors of the American Civic Association.[59]

She continued to work for abolition of the poorhouse system and for old age pensions. In 1933, Crane was named chairman of the Michigan Association for Old Age Security.[60] She had founded the Kalamazoo chapter of the organization, believing that a system of pensions for the elderly was important in the process of dismantling the poorhouse system. In the 1930s Michigan still had eighty-one poorhouses with five thousand patients. Most were destitute elderly.[61] In 1933, Crane wrote a play entitled "Old Folks at Home," which showed the conditions in Michigan almshouses and which was presented to the 1934 state convention of Business and Professional Women meeting in Kalamazoo.[62]

Crane's final civic project in 1932 grew out of the necessity of replacing Kalamazoo County's antiquated jail.[63] She had become convinced that few offenders were improved by imprisonment, a method of punishment that, she believed, should be reserved for only the hardened criminal. Other offenders, she felt, particularly the young, should be placed on penal farms.

Characteristically, Crane, who was in her seventies, made personal investigations of several prisons and penal farms to prepare a report for the County Board of Supervisors. Her visits included the Indiana State Penal Farm at Greencastle, the Berks County Penitentiary and Penal Farm near Philadelphia, the Detroit House of Correction, and the Jackson (Michigan) State Prison

Farms. Crane hoped to interest Michigan in developing a state-wide network of penal farms.[64]

The County Board of Supervisors gave preliminary approval to Crane's idea, and William E. Upjohn of the Upjohn Company donated 230 acres for the Kalamazoo penal farm site. But Crane's proposal was never approved. Residents near the proposed site opposed the project and federal money became available for a new courthouse and jail.[65]

Crane's contributions to her city, state, and nation were recognized at an appreciation dinner at People's Church on May 17, 1934, following the unveiling at the Kalamazoo Public Library of a bas-relief of her image created by Chicago sculptor C. Warner Williams. The inscription on the sculpture, which remains today at the library, reads "Citizen-Minister-Scholar."[66] This recognition was sponsored by the Kalamazoo Business and Professional Women's Club, of which Crane was an active member. Earlier in her life she had been accorded honorary doctorate degrees from Carthage College, her alma mater[67] and by Kalamazoo College (1917).[68] But the appreciation dinner was the community's only tribute to Crane.

On the evening of March 24, 1935, Crane, at seventy-six years of age, was unable to sleep. Following a habit of many years, she had started down the stairs of her home to her study when she was stricken by a heart attack. She fell down the stairs and was dead when physicians arrived. Funeral services were held at her beloved People's Church and her body was buried in Homewood Cemetery in Kalamazoo.[69] Her husband joined her in death two years later.[70]

The *Kalamazoo Gazette*, in an editorial, noted Crane's contributions to her community, and the honor and the prestige she had brought the city through her efforts in far broader fields. The newspaper found it impossible to list all of her accomplish-

Text on the bas-relief:

·CAROLINE·BARTLETT·CRANE·
CITIZEN—MINISTER—SCHOLAR
A TRIBUTE FROM HER FRIENDS
MAY   —•—   1934

22.

Bas-relief of Caroline Bartlett Crane, by Chicago sculptor C. Warner
Williams (Regional History Collection, WMU Archives).

ments. "One may safely say that no sound and substantial movement to better the condition of mankind lacked Dr. Crane's
helpful interest, and that most such movements enjoyed her
enthusiastic support," the editorial said. It continued:

> Yet for all her broadness of vision and devotion to the
> advancement of humanity on a worldwide scale, Dr. Crane, as
> all of us know so well, reserved a special place in her heart for
> the affairs of the community she called home. In spirit and in
> outlook a true citizen of the world, she was yet able to serve
> brilliantly and enthusiastically as a leading citizen of
> Kalamazoo.

Crane's selflessness was also noted. "In reference to Dr. Crane it
can be said with an exceptional degree of truth and accuracy that
here was a leader who asked no reward other than the satisfaction
of helpful service to others."[71]

In 1985, fifty five years later, Crane's name gained
another measure of fame when she was named to the Michigan
Women's Hall of Fame.[72] Few women in American history lived
such a diverse and exciting life as Caroline Bartlett Crane, and few
contributed as much in so many ways to their nation, state, and
local community. Crane was an outstanding public speaker, a
journalist, a suffragette, an urban health and municipal consultant,
a social reformer, a charity expert, a housing reformer, and a
patriot. Most of all—as the inscription on the bas-relief reads—she
was a minister and citizen. Caroline Bartlett Crane achieved
satisfaction through good works in her community, state, and
nation, and to acknowledge her contributions is the just verdict of
history.

NOTES

[1]J. Stanley Lemons, *The Woman Citizen*, pp. 14–17.

[2]Lemons, *The Woman Citizen*, pp. 14–17.

[3]Lemons, *The Woman Citizen*, pp. 10–16.

[4]Caroline Bartlett Crane to officers of the Woman's Committee of the Council of National Defense (Michigan Division) 15 July 1919, Crane Papers. (The letter also was published under the title "The Passing of Ann Howard Shaw," which was printed by the Anna Howard Shaw Memorial, Michigan Headquarters, Detroit, Michigan.)

[5]"Mrs. J. E. Crane Dies in Kazoo," newspaper clipping ca. April 1920, Crane Papers, and various biographical materials in Crane Papers.

[6]Crane, "Parenthood" in 1934 typescript recollections, Crane Papers; and Huyser, "A. D. Crane, M.D.," p. 12.

[7]Caroline Bartlett Crane to Augustus Warren Crane, 20 November 1918, Crane Papers.

[8]Caroline Bartlett Crane to Augustus Warren Crane, 8 July 1928, Crane Papers; and Caroline Bartlett Crane to Augustus Warren Crane, 10 July 1928, Crane Papers.

[9]Augustus Warren Crane to Caroline Bartlett Crane, 4 May 1922, Crane Papers; and Roscoe Hildreth, "From X-Ray Martyrs to Low Level Radiation," a pamphlet published by the author, Kalamazoo, Michigan, p. 15.

[10]Caroline Bartlett Crane to Augustus Warren Crane, 17 April 1922, Crane Papers.

[11]Interview, Juliana B. Crane, Orlando, Florida, 6 December 1985.

[12]"Mrs. Caroline B. Crane Suffers Great Pain," *Kalamazoo Gazette* (26 December 1924).

[13]"Dr. Caroline Bartlett Crane," *The Michigan Business Women's Bulletin* (July 1934), p. 12.

[14]"Biographical Sketch," p. 18, Crane Papers.

[15]"Kalamazoo County League of Women Voters Studying International Cooperation to Prevent War," *Kalamazoo Gazette* (12 February 1933); and "Several Clubs Sponsor Talks by Mrs. Crane," *Flint Journal* (4 March 1929).

[16]"WVL Hears Attack on War as Stupidity," unidentified Kalamazoo newspaper, undated, Crane Papers. In this article, Crane reports on her participation in the American Peace Association Conference in Cleveland. She said the APA was a "middle of the road peace organization."

[17]"Says Defeat of League of Nations Would Be Death Blow to America's Respect," *Kalamazoo Gazette*, undated, Crane Papers.

[18]Charles DeBenedetti, *Origins of the Peace Movement, 1915–1929* (Millwood, N.Y.: KTO Press, 1978), pp. 96, 153; and Mary Gray Peck, *Carrie Chapman Catt: A Biography* (New York: H. W. Wildon Company, 1944), pp. 409–11.

[19]Crane, "Conference on Cause and Cure of War," in 1934 typescript recollections, p. 1, Crane Papers.

[20]Lemons, *The Woman Citizen*, pp. 50–51.

[21]*U. S. House of Representatives, Hearings Before the Committee on Public Buildings and Grounds on House Resolution 7014*, a bill to create a Bureau of Housing and Living Conditions in the Department of Labor, 12 November 1919, pp. 6–7; "Housing Experts Favor Federal Aid," *Washington Post* (12 November 1919); and "Endorse Bill for Housing Bureau in Labor Department," *Washington Star* (12 November 1919). (Hereafter, the hearing resolution will be referred to as *Housing Bill Proceedings*.)

[22]*Housing Bill Proceedings*, p. 7.

[23]Lemons, *The Woman Citizen*, p. 253.

[24]Caroline Bartlett Crane, "Clean Streets," *Woman Citizen*, n.s. 8 (8 March 1924), pp. 10–11; Caroline Bartlett Crane, "Making Garbage Respectable," *Woman Citizen*, n.s. 8 (5 April 1924), p. 13; and Caroline Bartlett Crane, "Doing Something About Smoke," *Woman Citizen*, n.s. 8 (17 May 1924), p. 12.

[25]"Dr. C. B. Crane Is Named On Staff Of N. Y. Magazine," *Kalamazoo Gazette* (12 April 1925).

[26]Caroline Bartlett Crane, "Small Town Tenements," *Woman Citizen*, n.s. 10 (August 1925), p. 11.

[27]Caroline Bartlett Crane, "Suburbs Beyond the Law," *Woman Citizen*, n.s. 10 (September 1925), p. 12.

[28]Caroline Bartlett Crane, "Slums of the Countryside," *Woman Citizen,* n.s. 10 (October 1925), p. 15.

[29]Caroline Bartlett Crane, "Cow and the Baby," *Woman Citizen*, n.s. 10 (December 1925), pp. 18–19; and Caroline Bartlett Crane, "Does Your Town Need a Mr. Ward," *Woman Citizen*, n.s. 10 (February 1926), p. 17.

[30]Caroline Bartlett Crane, "Jury Service in a Michigan City," *Woman's Journal*, n.s. 12 (November 1927), p. 27; Caroline Bartlett Crane, "Women Ascend the Pulpit," *Woman's Journal*, n.s. 14 (December 1929), pp. 14–16; and Caroline Bartlett Crane, "Future Forest Primeval," *Woman Citizen*, n.s. 11 (January 1927), pp. 14–16.

[31]Caroline Bartlett Crane with foreword by Herbert Hoover, *Everyman's House* (Garden City, N.Y.: Doubleday, Page & Company, 1925), p. 3.

[32]Crane, *Everyman's House*, p. 3.

[33]Herbert Hoover to Caroline Bartlett Crane, 23 October 1924, Crane Papers.

[34]Blanche Brace, "A Home Built Around a Mother," *Delineator* (February 1912), p. 2.

[35]Brace, "A Home Built Around a Mother," p. 2.

[36]Crane, *Everyman's House,* p. 6.

[37]Herbert Hoover to Caroline Bartlett Crane, 25 June 1924, Crane Papers.

[38]"Mother's Comfort is Plan Aim," *American Builder* (October 1924), 98–100; and Brace, "A Home Built Around a Mother," p. 2.

[39]Crane, *Everyman's House*, p. 43.

[40]Brace, "A Home Built Around a Mother."

[41]Caroline Bartlett Crane, "Advantages of Kalamazoo Better Home Told in Detail," flier reprinted from article appearing in *Kalamazoo Gazette* (12 May 1924).

[42]Caroline Bartlett Crane to Lyman Beecher Stowe, 25 February 1927, Crane Papers; and numerous other letters exchanged between Crane and Stowe between 1925 and 1927.

[43]Program 1929–30 Michigan Housing Association, Crane Papers; "Lauds Backers of Pedigreed House," *Kalamazoo Gazette* (20 September 1928); and "Housing Society Honors Mrs. Crane," *Kalamazoo Gazette* (3 March 1928).

[44]"Mrs. Crane Re-elected to Board of Directors," *Kalamazoo Gazette* (30 September 1928); Virginia M. Straith to Caroline Bartlett Crane, 28 September 1934, Crane Papers; and "Named Associate Member of the Academy of Medicine," *Kalamazoo Gazette* (12 March 1928).

[45]"Caroline Bartlett Crane Discusses WTCU Endorsement," *Kalamazoo Gazette* (7 November 1928).

[46]Lemons, *The Woman Citizen*, pp. 207–25.

[47]Caroline Bartlett Crane to Dr. Harriette McCalmont Stone, 28 May 1928, Crane Papers.

[48]Caroline Bartlett Crane to Dr. Harriette McCalmont Stone, 28 May 1928, Crane Papers.

[49]Signed statement by Harriette McCalmont Stone and her daughter, Helen Stone McColle, addressed to the regent of the Lucinda Hillsdale Stone chapter of the Daughters of the American Revolution, 13 June 1928.

[50]Caroline Bartlett Crane to Augustus Warren Crane, 10 July 1928, Crane Papers.

[51]Caroline Bartlett Crane to Augustus Warren Crane, 10 July 1928, Crane Papers.

[52]"Charles Bartlett Dies," unidentified newspaper, 30 November 1928, Crane Papers.

[53]Caroline Bartlett Crane to Augustus Warren Crane, 13 August 1931, Crane Papers.

[54]Caroline Bartlett Crane to Augustus Warren Crane, 2 June 1934, Crane Papers.

[55]Caroline Bartlett Crane to Augustus Warren Crane, three letters: 28 August 1932, 11 September 1932, and 21 September 1932, Crane Papers.

[56]"Mayor Names 28 on Committee to Assist Jobless," *Kalamazoo Gazette* (13 December 1930).

[57]"Biographical Sketch," p. 18, Crane Papers.

[58]*Who's Who in America,* s. v. "Caroline Bartlett Crane," vol. 18, 1934–35 ed., p. 626.

[59]*Cyclopaedia of American Biographies,* s. v. "Caroline Bartlett Crane," vol. 15, 1916 ed., p. 64.

[60]"Caroline B. Crane Heads State Old Age Pension Body," *Kalamazoo Gazette* (15 February 1933).

[61]"Caroline B. Crane Heads State Old Age Pension Body."

[62]Caroline Bartlett Crane, "Old Folks at Home," unpublished manuscript in Crane Papers; and Program of the 1932 meeting of the Michigan Federation of Business and Professional Women, 26 May 1932, Crane Papers.

[63]"Let Minor Offenders Work on Penal Farm and Support Themselves," *Kalamazoo Gazette* (28 June 1932).

[64]"Supervisor Board Hears Penal Farm Report," *Kalamazoo Gazette* (28 June 1932).

[65]"Prison Farm Site Will Be Given County," *Kalamazoo Gazette* (8 January 1932), Crane Papers; and "Supervisors Ask $730,000 Federal Loan," *Kalamazoo Gazette* (10 August 1933).

[66]"Tribute Paid to C. B. Crane by Community," *Kalamazoo Gazette* (18 May 1934).

[67]"Carthage Honors Caroline B. Crane," *Kalamazoo Gazette* (4 January 1926).

[68]*Kalamazoo College Bulletin* 13 (1917–18), 84, Kalamazoo College Archives. Crane's family members also engaged success in life. Juliana later became an x-ray technician in her father's office. Their son, Bartlett, received his bachelor's degree from Antioch College and later became a physician in Kalamazoo after graduation from Rush Medical College in Chicago. Warren published nearly forty professional papers, and for their literary value he received an honorary Master of Arts degree from the University of Michigan.

[69]"Caroline Bartlett Crane," *New York Times* (25 March 1935).

[70]"Dr. Augustus W. Crane Dies Suddenly," *Kalamazoo Gazette* (20 February 1937).

[71]"Caroline Bartlett Crane," *Kalamazoo Gazette* (25 March 1935).

[72]"America's Housekeeper Due for Hall of Fame Induction," *Kalamazoo Gazette* (8 February 1985).

INDEX

Taft, William Howard, 236
Talbot, Marion, 6
Thomas, Rev. Hiram, 68, 74
Toynbee House, 61
Tressler, Dr. D. L., 27, 29, 30, 31
Twain, Mark (Samuel Clemens), 2, 33-34
Twentieth Century Club, 76, 117, 120-21, 127

Unitarianism, 5, 45-46, 51-53, 65-56
Unity Club, 52, 80
Universalism, 24, 46, 48, 74
University of Chicago, 4-6, 80, 96
Upjohn, William E., 250

Viola, The, 16, 20-21

Wagner, Adolph, 5
Warner, Charles Dudley, 2
Warner, Gov. Fred M., 149
Waring, George E., 4, 129
Washington, Booker, T., 207
Western Issue, 51, 53, 55
Western Unitarian Conference, 5, 51, 65, 68
Wholesome Meat Act of 1967, 210-11
Wiley, Dr. Harvey W., 145, 191, 196, 199
Wilkes, Rev. Eliza Tupper, 48
Williams, Charles Aft, 32-33, 36
Williams, C. Warner, 250
Wilson, James, 145, 148, 210
Wilson, Woodrow, 208, 222, 226
Woman Citizen (*Woman's Journal*), 241-42
Woman's Congress, 7
Woman's Work in Municipalities, 8
Women's Christian Temperance Union (WCTU), 35, 53, 76, 77-78, 240, 246
Women's Congress of Representative Women, 73
Women's Disease Syndrome, 183-84
Women's Liberal League, 63
Women's Ministerial Conference, 54, 58
Women's Peace Party, 221
World Parliament of Religions, 73

ZY Circulars, 196-98

DATE DUE
